How To Be a
Successful Philanthropist

Avoiding the Legal Pitfalls

by

Bruce R. Hopkins

DORRANCE
PUBLISHING CO
EST. 1920
PITTSBURGH, PENNSYLVANIA 15238

Dorrance Publishing Co
585 Alpha Drive
Pittsburgh, PA 15238
Visit our website at www.dorrancebookstore.com

ISBN: 978-1-4809-9916-9
eISBN: 978-1-4809-9934-3

Contents

What is a Philanthropist?

Three Cases

What Do You Want to Do?

The Choices Are Yours

Now You Are Ready To Be a Philanthropist

Priorities

Looking Ahead

Charitable Organizations

Educational Organizations

Scientific Organizations

Religious Organizations

Application Process

Other Charity Law

What is a *Private Foundation*?

Disqualified Persons

Governance of Foundations

What do Foundations Do?

Private Operating Foundations

Preface

This book arose out of an aspect of my law practice. For nearly 50 years, I have been representing nonprofit, tax-exempt organizations, with an emphasis on charitable entities. Thus, my work has principally been serving charitable organizations and their governing boards. There have been deviations from this model, such as performing services for fundraising companies, but they have been rare.

This type of law practice necessarily involves advice and assistance in forming nonprofit organizations. Generally, I have been doing this from a "corporate" standpoint, which is to say focusing on the type of entity, its governing documents, its governance policies, the application for recognition of tax exemption (if any), its reporting obligations, compliance with the federal tax laws, and other similar aspects. Usually, I have not been that much involved in the funding of the organization (other than advising as to public charity status).

In recent years, however, there has been a discernible shift in the emphasis of my practice. More frequently now, individuals are coming to me, seeking advice as to how to be more actively engaged in charitable undertakings. This desire to "give back" is usually stimulated by a somewhat sudden accretion of funds— an inheritance, selling of a business, even winning a lottery. These individuals may not always use the word, but they are seeking a way (or perhaps ways) to become a *philanthropist*.

This may be a good place for an unavoidable digression. Obviously, it takes money to be a philanthropist. The more money that is available, the more good that can be done. Not being trained in matters financial, and not otherwise equipped with an affinity for the skill, I am of little help in assisting individuals in accumulating wealth. An investment advisor I am not. Thus, this book is not titled *How To Become a Successful Philanthropist.* For help on getting the money, you will have to turn elsewhere. I pick up where and when the funds show up.

Back to the main theme. This book is designed to show the budding philanthropist the best way forward. There are ample tools for success out there—principally, the private foundation, the supporting organization, other forms of public charities, the donor-advised fund, and the charitable remainder trust. The trick is to understand how to manipulate (in the best sense of that term) these devices. The point of the book is to provide that understanding.

In addition to chapters on each of these tools, I have included illustrations, questions, and checklists in an effort to go beyond the technicalities of and pitfalls in the law and illuminate the philanthropist's path to rewarding charitable giving. Certainly, the approaches will not always be the same. The pleasure of the practice is to match the tool or tools most appropriate in a particular case to the needs and wants of the client, to enable these individuals to satisfy their goals and maximize their charitable giving experience.

I have tried to capture that pleasure in this book. I'll conclude this Preface with the conclusion in the book: Happy and productive giving!

Bruce R. Hopkins

June, 2018

Introduction

Bruce R. Hopkins gave me the opportunity to read *How To Be a Successful Philanthropist* before it went to press. Coming from a fundraising and development background, I quickly came to the conclusion that this book will not only be invaluable to the philanthropist but also for fundraising and development professionals. Bruce is a well-known, highly respected lawyer specializing in tax-exempt organizations and charitable giving and has authored numerous books focusing on the area of the law and how it relates to tax-exempt organizations. I consider this book a "must read" for anyone who is considering becoming a philanthropist or for anyone who already is a philanthropist.

The information Bruce has provided in *How To Be a Successful Philanthropist* details the various vehicles for giving, including illustrations, advantages and disadvantages for each, and what to look out for from a legal standpoint. He informs the reader about the rules and regulations for charitable giving and for tax-exempt organizations. If you are a fundraising and development professional, this book provides you with the tools to have an in-depth conversation with your donors or prospective donors about how they might want to consider making a gift to your organization. I've not read a book that provides essential information for both the donor and the donee before reading *How To Be a Successful Philanthropist*. This book should be a ready reference on your desk.

Dianne D. Day
President
DDD Consulting, Inc.
San Diego, California

Chapter 1
Setting the Stage

Let's first consider the fundamental matter of the applicable meaning of the word *philanthropist*. Then, as an introduction to the subsequent chapters, a list of the fundamental questions exploring what the budding philanthropist wants to do—from a law standpoint—is provided. For the philanthropist planning on establishing a charitable organization, another checklist is provided summarizing the steps for getting started.

What is a Philanthropist?

The word *philanthropist* has several meanings. Before getting to them, however, it should be noted at the outset—since this book is written from the perspective of a lawyer—that the words *philanthropy, philanthropic*, and *philanthropist* are not formally recognized in the law. The word that has that august perch is *charitable*. But, while the words *charitable* and *philanthropic* are somewhat synonymous, the English language fails us in this regard otherwise. One who gives large sums of money to charity is not a *charitablist*. Matters worsen: try working with *eleemosynary*.

Consequently, when describing charitably disposed individuals, the word *philanthropist* lingers on, despite its lack of formality in the law. The principal definition of *philanthropist*—and the one used in this book—is an individual who contributes large sums of money for charitable purposes. Other definitions of the term include individuals who administer large amounts of charitable dollars given by others, such as a president or trustee of a charitable trust, or those who volunteer considerable amounts of time for charitable objectives.

The charitable fundraising community has this all figured out. A typical fundraising consultant will differentiate between those who contribute "time, treasure, and talent." Those who give their time and/or talent to charity, such as by serving on charities' boards or being officers of charities, are, in their way, philanthropists. But not for the purposes of this book. We are concerned only with those who are planning to give, or who have already started giving, their treasure.

Thinking about philanthropists (using this book's definition of the term) conjures surnames like Bloomberg, Branson, Buffett, Carnegie, Ford, Gates, Hughes, Koch, Rockefeller, Soros, and Vanderbilt. They have given, and some still are giving, billions of dollars to charity. But individuals can give much less and still be considered philanthropists—as we will see.

Three Cases

Steve and Mary Smith, a married couple, ages 50 and 45, have built a successful business over 25 years. They have two children, Molly and Polly, ages 20 and 18. Steve and Mary have just liquidated their business and want to devote the proceeds of sale of the business to the support of their favorite charitable pursuits. The sale of the business has netted them $10 million.

Peter and Sally Brown, a married couple, ages 50 and 45, have two children, James and Jessica, ages 20 and 18. Peter and Sally have just inherited $50 million. They want to quit their jobs and devote the remainder of their lives to their favorite charitable pursuits.

Carl and Nancy Jones, a married couple, ages 50 and 45, have two children, Robert and Priscilla, ages 20 and 18. Carl and Nancy have just won $100 million (net of taxes) in a lottery, thanks to Nancy's purchase, on a last-minute whim, of the winning ticket. They want to quit their jobs and devote the remainder of their lives to their favorite charitable pursuits.

These vignettes are not uncommon. The three mini-narratives have been made as similar as possible. There are three important differences in the facts. One difference is largely irrelevant to our concerns: the source of the cash that the couples now have at their disposal. The second difference is very important for our purposes and also quite obvious: the amount of money involved. The third difference is the duration of the use of the funds for charity: immediate or life-long.

What Do You Want to Do?

Each of these couples has come to me, seeking legal advice as to the best way, from their standpoint, to devote these funds to charity. Without answering the following questions at this point, or even passing judgment on them, here are the basic questions I asked them at our initial meeting:

- How much money are they planning on giving to charity, now and in the future?
- Are there any properties other than money to be contributed to charity?
- Will any of these funds be invested? If so, what is the anticipated annual return?
- What are their priorities as to the funding of charitable causes?
- Do they want to contribute their charitable dollars on one or a few occasions?
- Do either or both of them want to institutionalize their giving by creating a charity?
- Do they have any ideas as to the form of this charity?
- How about more than one charity?
- Do they have any ideas about the forms of these charities?
- Do either or both of them want to participate in the governance of a charity, such as being a board member or an officer?
- Do either or both of them want to be an employee of a charity?
- Do either or both of their children want to participate in the governance of a charity?
- Do either or both of their children want to be an employee of a charity?
- Do either or both of them want to control a charity?
- Do they have other family members and/or friends they want to involve in their charitable activities?
- Do they want charitable deductions for their gifts? (The answer to this one is usually obvious.)
- Do they want an income flow as the result of their gifts?
- How do these charitable interests interrelate with their overall financial plans?
- How do these charitable interests interrelate with their estate plan?

The Choices Are Yours
Here is the list of options I laid out for each of these couples as to use of their funds for charitable purposes, leaving aside for the moment the not-inconsequential matter of the federal tax implications:

- Give all the money away to charity immediately, with no further involvement.
- Give the money away immediately and become a board member or officer of one or more of the charitable recipients.
- Give the money away immediately and become an employee of one of the charitable recipients.
- Give the money away immediately, with one or both of the children becoming a board member of one or more of the charitable recipients.
- Give the money away immediately, with one or both or the children becoming an employee of one of the charitable recipients.
- Create one or more charities to receive the charitable contributions.
- If the foregoing option is selected, will a charity be a public or private one?
- If a charity is created, will one or more of the donors serve on its board?
- If a charity is created, will one or more of the donors' children serve on its board?
- If a charity is created, will one or more of the donors be an employee of it?
- If a charity is created, will one or more of the donors' children be an employee of it?
- Utilize one or more donor-advised funds.
- Utilize a charitable remainder trust and/or charitable gift annuity.
- Retain some of the funds and contribute them from one or both of the decedent's estates.
- Combine two or more of these options.

Now You Are Ready To Be a Philanthropist

Use of any of these options makes an individual a philanthropist—that is, a lover of humankind. (Or, if you prefer, you can be an altruist or a humanitarian.) A philanthropist is an individual who engages in one or more acts of generosity as evidenced by contributions of money or other property for charitable ends. (Sometimes, although I find it awkward, the word *philanthropy* is used to describe a charitable organization.)

For our purposes, there are two types of philanthropists. One type is the one-shot philanthropist who simply gives it all away at one time. For example, Steve and Mary could give the $10 million to charity today and be done with the matter (other than enjoying multiple years of charitable contribution deductions). The other type of philanthropist is the one who creates a charitable organization, and perhaps one or more other entities, and spends years administering the organization(s) and distributing (spending) funds for charitable purposes and otherwise furthering charitable objectives.

Within the constraints of funds available, the choice of type of philanthropist is yours.

Priorities

Based on nearly 50 years of practicing nonprofit law, I can say without equivocation that the first and highest priority of the philanthropist should be concern with the charitable pursuits. The other stuff may be important but not the most important. What other stuff? Matters such as board service, employment, and charitable deductions.

For example, service on the board of one or more charities is a noteworthy expenditure of one's time, but it ought not be done to network for clients or advance in social circles or otherwise enhance one's reputation. Board service, if done right, is hard and time-consuming work. A trustee or director of a charity is, after all, a fiduciary. The task carries with it many duties, including a duty of care (prudence) and loyalty to the organization, and responsibilities—not to mention some risk of personal legal liability. A charity directorship should not be a sinecure, a place where the occupant of the position every now and then receives committee reports, then goes to lunch and otherwise basks in the glory of being a board member. All of this also pertains to service as an officer of a charity.

Although it is frequently done, forming a charity for the purpose of creating one or more positions of employment, for the founder and/or one or more family members is, well, bad form. This outcome is best achieved as a byproduct of truly charitable motives. In any event, whatever you do, when applying to the IRS for recognition of tax exemption (see Chapter 2), please don't say that the principal purpose in forming the charity is to provide employment for the family!

As for the charitable contribution deductions, they will come about as a matter of law, although there is planning that can be done to maximize them (see Chapter 7).

So the philanthropist should set some priorities as to charitable ends. Much of this will be dictated by the amount of money available for charitable objectives. Another, somewhat-related element is the "impact" factor. The philanthropist may want to heavily support one or two charitable causes or spray money around in support of dozens of charities. Some donors like to concentrate on financially assisting a single institution, such as a college, hospital, or religious institution, while others send smaller amounts of money out to any number of worthy causes. (The legal framework for this decision-making is in Chapter 2.)

It may be that the most the philanthropist can do is confine the largess to a field of charity, such as combating poverty, making scholarship grants, improving health care, or supporting the arts. Law does not mandate this type of priorities setting; it is simply a matter of good funds management. The philanthropist may want to reduce this boundary-setting exercise to writing, such as a mission statement. This is often done where the charitable giving is institutionalized, such as use of private foundations or donor-advised funds. A byproduct of this form of establishment of priorities is that grant seekers who are outside the funding frame can be gracefully turned away with a simple decline such as: "We're sorry, but your project, worthy as it is, is outside the scope of our funding priorities."

Looking Ahead

If your plans include forming a charitable organization, whether public or private, here is a ten-point checklist to get you started:

1. *The form of the organization.* You have four choices: nonprofit corporation, trust, unincorporated association, and limited liability company. The latter two types of entities are unlikely candidates. In my opinion, the best of this selection is the nonprofit corporation. There are several reasons for this view. One is the fact that the corporate form almost always provides an effective shield against personal liability for the organization's directors and officers. (Sure, insurance can be purchased and indemnifications created, but why take the chance?) Another reason is the fact that the nonprofit corporation is the best known and understood of the foursome. A third reason: just about every state has a nonprofit corporation act; this statute (and accompanying regulations and case law) will answer many questions about the organization's governance and other operations, such as the number of directors, required officer positions, length of terms, meetings requirements, voting rights, and committees.

2. *The name of the organization.* This will depend in large part on its program activities. If the charity is to be a private foundation, it will probably have a name such as the Peter and Sally Brown Foundation. Or, if the entire family is going to be involved, something along the lines of the Carl and Nancy White Family Foundation. If the entity is to be a public charity, it should take on a name more descriptive of its type, although some supporting organizations have names similar to private foundations.

3. *The location of the organization.* Generally, the charity will be formed in the state in which its founders live. There may be a good reason to establish the entity

elsewhere, but that's unlikely. Also, a charity may engage in its program activities in more than one state. (The home state is the organization's *domicile*; the other state or states are *foreign* ones.)

4. *The address of the organization*. Please try to find some office space, no matter how meager. Which is to say, don't attempt to operate the charity out of your home.

5. *The governing documents of the organization*. Every nonprofit organization, including a charitable one, is formed by the creation and, usually, filing of a document. Yes, some charities are formed by statute, but that approach is rare. The legal term for this formative document is *articles of organization*. Examples are articles of incorporation and declarations of trust. Another document is the operating rules of the entity, commonly termed *bylaws*. Please spend a little money and have these documents prepared by a competent nonprofit lawyer. The fees can be paid by the charity.

6. *The application for recognition of exemption*. This document is discussed in the next chapter. This is an important document, warranting careful and thorough (and accurate) preparation. Again, this application should be prepared with the assistance of competent legal counsel. Particular attention should be paid to crafting the statement of purposes and the summary of the activities of the organization. This will be money well spent.

7. *Annual information returns*. The charity will be filing annual information returns with the IRS. Please find your way to a competent accountant who will assist in the preparation and filing of these documents. Please also have these returns reviewed by a competent lawyer before they are filed. (You may be surprised at the number of times I have been asked to review these returns—after they have been filed. This legal assistance is much more effective if received before the filing with the IRS.)

8. *Policies*. These days, much more documentation than articles of organization and bylaws is required of charitable organizations, especially public charities. We are in the age of policies (thanks to the IRS). The types of policies will vary, depending on the type and size of the organization. At a minimum, the following policies should be considered: conflict-of-interest, document retention and destruction, whistleblower, investment, and travel and other expenses reimbursement.

9. *Recordkeeping and substantiation*. The federal tax law imposes recordkeeping requirements that must be followed if a charitable deduction or deductions are desired. Likewise, availability of the charitable deduction depends on compliance with gift substantiation (perhaps including appraisal) rules. Just because you are the founder of a charity doesn't mean you don't have to comply with these rules. If the

choice is to give all the money away to charity, the donor—to obtain the otherwise available charitable deduction or deductions—should obtain the properly phrased substantiation document from the charity or charities. Steve and Mary don't want to lose their $10 million in charitable deductions (or whatever the deductible amount turns out to be) for lack of the necessary written words. More on this in Chapter 7.

10. Going forward. As the years go by, keep up the relationships with competent lawyers and accountants. They will answer questions about operations, help develop grant agreements, assist in the preparation of annual reports, and keep the charitable organization apprised of pertinent developments in nonprofit law, particularly the federal tax law. This is not the place for do-it-yourself.

Chapter 2

Charity and the Law

The phrase *charitable organization* is used, in the federal tax law, in two ways. One, it is used to describe all organizations referenced in famous Internal Revenue Code section 501(c)(3), including educational, scientific, and religious entities. This is because—with one minor exception for organizations that test for public safety—all these categories of organizations are eligible to receive deductible charitable contributions. Two, it is used in a more technical sense, referencing as many as 30 ways to be charitable.

A philanthropist, potential or actual, should make an effort to inventory the types of programs warranting funding, either directly or by means of the philanthropist's charity, and match them up with one or more of the law's categories of charitable undertakings. There is plenty to pick from.

Charitable Organizations

The types of activities that qualify as *charitable* ones (in the technical sense), for federal tax purposes, are referenced in the tax regulations, IRS revenue rulings, or court opinions. These are not rigid classifications; there can be overlaps. For example, an organization providing scholarships can be simultaneously relieving the underprivileged and advancing education.

The following are the types of activities that can be undertaken as charitable enterprises, usually by public charities, or that can be funded by grants from charitable organizations, the typical province of private foundations. (These entities are the subject of Chapters 3 and 5.)

Relief of the Poor

The relief of poverty is the most basic and historically founded form of charitable activity. Those who are poor constitute, for that reason alone, members of a charitable class. Organizations that are charitable by reason of this category usually provide services, such as vocational training, low-income housing, legal services, furnishing of meals, transportation services, and the like. Of course, direct financial assistance may also be provided.

Relief of the Distressed

An individual may be distressed without simultaneously being poor, although there is a fine line between someone who is poor and someone who is financially distressed. Individuals may also be physically distressed or emotionally distressed without necessarily being poor. This is the basis for charitable status for various forms of disaster relief and hardship programs.

Relief of the Underprivileged

This category of charitable undertakings generally involves the performance of services along the lines of services for the poor. Additional types of services for the underprivileged include money management advice and scholarships.

Advancement of Education

Another way to be charitable is to advance education, which can be confusing since being educational is a separate basis for tax exemption and gift deductibility. Programs in this category include forms of student assistance such as scholarships and fellowships, the making of awards, types of research, various publications, salary supplement programs, and the operation of conferences and seminars.

Advancement of Religion

Confusion can also arise in this context because activities that are religious in nature are a discrete basis for tax exemption, as is advancement of religion. This type of charitable activity includes the construction and maintenance of monuments and burial grounds, dissemination of religious literature, salary supplement programs, and the conduct of religious retreats.

Advancement of Science

Just as programs that are considered scientific qualify for tax exemption, so too are programs that are charitable because they advance science. Again, activities that qualify under this category include the financing of scholarships and fellowships, the making of awards, dissemination of publications, and the operation of conferences and seminars.

Lessening the Burdens of Government

One of the more traditional ways to be charitable is to engage in activities that lessen the burdens of one or more governments. This may be the most intriguing of the concepts of what is charitable because governments have broad latitude in determining what they do and the burdens they assume. Once that standard is met, activities that could never qualify under any other rationale can be regarded as charitable.

The first step in this analysis is to determine whether an organization's activities are functions that pertain to objectives that a governmental body considers to be its burden. The second step is to ascertain whether these activities in fact lessen a government's burden. The IRS requires a showing of an "objective manifestation" by a government that it considers the activity to be lessening one or more of its burdens. It is insufficient that an organization engages in an activity that is sometimes undertaken by a government or that a government or governmental official expresses approval of an organization and its activities.

Some organizations that are tax-exempt under this category of charitable provide services directly in the context of governmental activity, such as assisting in the preservation of a public lake, beautifying a city, assisting in the operation of a mass transportation system, maintaining a volunteer fire company, and encouraging plantings of public lands. Matters can get wilder, with charities, under this rubric, operating convention centers, hotels, theaters, aquariums, conservatories, and sports teams.

Promotion of Social Welfare

The promotion of social welfare is one of the more indefinite categories of charitable purposes. The law breaks this one down into five categories: activities (1) designed to accomplish any of the foregoing charitable activities, (2) that lessen "neighborhood tensions," (3) that eliminate prejudice and discrimination, (4) that defend human and civil rights secured by law, and (5) that combat community deterioration and juvenile delinquency.

Promotion of Health

The promotion of health as a charitable purpose includes establishment and/or maintenance of hospitals, clinics, homes for the aged, and other providers of health care; advancement of medical and similar knowledge through research; and the maintenance of conditions conducive to health. Other types of organizations that fall within this category are medical research organizations, certain types of health maintenance organizations, fitness centers, blood banks, halfway houses, and accountable care organizations.

Promotion of the Arts

Organizations devoted to promotion of the arts may qualify for tax exemption as charitable entities, such as nonprofit theaters, symphonies, opera and ballet societies, and groups that promote appreciation of types of music. Other organizations of this genre are entities that make grants to needy artists, sponsor public exhibits of artwork by unknown yet promising artists, and train artists.

Environmental Protection

The IRS stated that it is "generally recognized that efforts to preserve and protect the natural environment for the benefit of the public serve a charitable purpose." Charitable entities exist that receive and maintain conservation easements and façade easements on historic properties.

Promotion of Patriotism

The promotion of patriotism is a charitable objective. Programs of this nature are those that "inculcate patriotic emotions," induce "civic pride," celebrate patriotic holidays, and promote displays of flags.

Promotion of Sports for Youth

The promotion, advancement, and sponsorship of recreational and amateur sports is a charitable activity. These organizations provide youth with learning facilities and educational programs that promote character development and life-enhancing values through sports.

Economic Development

Some types of economic development activities are charitable undertakings, often as a form of promotion of social welfare. This entails programs that provide low-cost financial assistance and similar aid designed to improve economic conditions and economic opportunities in economically depressed areas. More extensive forms of economic development may be charitable if undertaken as a lessening of the burden of a government.

Public Interest Law

Organizations structured as public interest law firms can qualify as charitable entities. These firms are nonprofit entities that provide legal representation in matters involving a broad public interest under circumstances where the financial interests at stake would not normally warrant representation from lawyers in private practice.

Sponsorship of Donor-Advised Funds

Organizations that sponsor donor-advised funds qualify as tax-exempt charitable entities. These funds are the subject of Chapter 4.

Fundraising for Charity

Charitable activity is considered to take place where contributions are made to an organization and that organization makes grants to other charities. The law focuses on the grantmaking component rather than the process used to generate the grant funds. The IRS applies a *commensurate test* to assess whether a charitable organization is maintaining grantmaking activities that are commensurate in scope with its financial resources. If the grantmaking is insufficient, the organization is not charitable.

More Overlapping

Some of these ways to be charitable overlap. For example, the operation of consortia, promotion of sports for youth, and facilitation of student and cultural exchanges are activities usually considered forms of advancement of education. Likewise, eligible economic development activities are often forms of promotion of social welfare and/or lessening the burdens of government.

Educational Organizations

The federal tax law does not contain a threshold, generic definition of the term *educational*; it rests on the concept that subjects spoken or written about must be objectively founded or developed. This is manifested in the *full and fair exposition test*, which permits materials that advocate a viewpoint to qualify as educational in nature but only if the advocacy is preceded by an objective discussion of the issue or subject involved. Thereafter, the IRS advanced a *methodology test*, pursuant to which a communication is evaluated by that agency to determine whether it is *educational*, as opposed to *propaganda*. In applying this test, the IRS is supposed to avoid any examination of the content of a communication (because of constitutional law considerations) and focus only on the method by which an advocate proceeds from the premises furnished to the conclusion advocated. If a communication is propaganda—that is, is the presentation of unsupported opinion—it cannot be educational.

Some tax-exempt organizations are clearly educational institutions. They include primary, secondary, and postsecondary schools and colleges and universities. These institutions have the required regularly scheduled curriculum, a regular faculty, and a regularly enrolled body of students in attendance at the place where the educational activities are regularly carried on. Other types of educational institutions include museums, planetariums, and symphony orchestras.

Education on just about any topic can be an exempt educational activity. This notion is essentially curbed only by principles of free speech and the public policy doctrine. Thus, the basic concept of *educational* as employed for federal tax law purposes is defined as relating to the "instruction or training of the individual for the purpose of improving or developing his capabilities" or the "instruction of the public on subjects useful to the individual and beneficial to the community."

Scientific Organizations

The Internal Revenue Code, the tax regulations, and IRS revenue rulings do not define the term *scientific* in the tax-exempt organizations context. A court stated that the term *science* means the "process by which knowledge is systematized or classified through the use of observation, experimentation, or reasoning." A fundamental requirement underlying this form of tax exemption is that the organization must serve a public rather than a private interest. Thus, an exempt scientific organization must, among the other criteria for exemption, be organized and operated in the public interest.

With tax-exempt scientific organizations, the focus is primarily on the concept of *research*. For research to be scientific, it must be carried on in furtherance of a scientific purpose. Thus, the term *scientific* includes the carrying on of scientific research in the public interest. The term *research* is not well-defined in the law. For purposes of the unrelated business income rules, for example, it is necessary to determine whether the organization is operated primarily for purposes of carrying on fundamental, as contrasted with applied, research. Scientific research does not include, however, activities ordinarily carried on incident to commercial operations, as, for example, the testing or inspection of materials or products or the designing or construction of equipment or buildings.

Scientific research is regarded as carried on in the public interest if the results of the research (including patents, copyrights, processes, or formulas) are made available to the public on a nondiscriminatory basis, if the research is performed for the

U.S. or its agencies and instrumentalities or for a state or political subdivision of a state, or if the research is directed toward benefiting the public. An organization is regarded as not organized or operated for the purpose of carrying on scientific research in the public interest and, consequently, will not qualify as a scientific organization for federal tax exemption purposes if (1) it performs research only for persons who are, directly or indirectly, its creators and not charitable organizations; or (2) it retains, directly or indirectly, the ownership or control of more than an insubstantial portion of the patents, copyrights, processes, or formulas resulting from its research and does not make the items available to the public on a nondiscriminatory basis.

Religious Organizations

With few exceptions, the IRS, other governmental agencies, and the courts have refused to or been quite cautious in attempting to define *religious* activities or organizations, or the word *religion*. Constitutional law constraints (the First Amendment's Religion Clauses) play a major role in this regard.

Decades ago, the Supreme Court grappled with the meaning of the term *religion*. It ventured the observation, authored well over a century ago, that the word has "reference to one's views of his relations to his Creator, and to the obligations they impose of reverence for his being and character, and of obedience to his will." Subsequently, the Court wrote that the "essence of religion is belief in a relation to God involving duties superior to those arising from any human relation." More recently, however, the Court stated that freedom of thought and religious belief "embraces the right to maintain theories of life and of death and of the hereafter which are rank heresy to followers of the orthodox faiths," and that, if triers of fact undertake to examine the truth or falsity of religious beliefs, "they enter a forbidden domain." The contemporary view among the judiciary on the topic is perhaps represented by this statement: "Neither this Court, nor any branch of this Government, will consider the merits or fallacies of a religion," nor will the court "compare the beliefs, dogmas, and practices of a newly organized religion with those of an older, more established religion," or "praise or condemn a religion, however excellent or fanatical or preposterous it may seem," because to do so "would impinge upon the guarantees of the First Amendment."

Within the realm of religious organizations are churches (including synagogues and mosques). A definition of the word *church* does not appear in the Internal Revenue Code or in the tax regulations. The IRS, in 1974, made public criteria (14 points) to be considered in determining whether a religious organization is a church for federal tax purposes; only "some" of the criteria need to be followed. Matters in this regard have changed dramatically, however, with the IRS drifting away from this multi-criteria approach and now insisting (in private letter rulings) that, for there to be an exempt church, there must be regular worship services conducted at a regular location with a regular congregation. (Thus, services by teleconference or online fail to qualify as church functions.) The IRS has been greatly aided in this regard by a court decision articulating a mandatory *associational test* as the standard for church status.

Other types of religious organizations recognized in the federal tax law are conventions and associations of churches, integrated auxiliaries of churches, mission societies, religious orders, apostolic organizations, communal groups, and retreat facilities.

Other Charitable Organizations

The realm of charitable organizations, from the standpoint of tax exemption, also includes organizations operating to prevent cruelty to children or animals, organizations that test for public safety, cooperative hospital organizations, cooperative educational service organizations, charitable risk pools, and endowments.

Application Process

With few exceptions, mostly involving churches and other religious organizations, an organization seeking to be a charitable entity is required to file an application for recognition of tax exemption with the IRS. This application, which is IRS Form 1023, solicits information about the applicant's proposed activities, governance, and finances. The IRS will rule adversely if the organization does not provide what the agency considers to be adequate information in support of the application. These applications are denied on a regular basis, with the IRS frequently applying the doctrines of private inurement, private benefit, and/or commerciality (see below). A favorable ruling recognizing tax exemption comes in the form of a *determination letter*.

The IRS also has a shorter application for recognition available for eligible organizations with revenues not in excess of $50,000. Thus, this type of entity will not be of much help to serious philanthropists. This application is on Form 1023-EZ.

A word about this matter of *recognition*. Contrary to the view of many, the IRS does not grant federal tax-exempt status to eligible charitable and other nonprofit organizations. Congress does that, by statute. Thus, if an organization qualifies for exemption, it is exempt; no regulatory agency can change that fact, including the

IRS. What the IRS does is *recognize* (or acknowledge) the existing exemption. (Most other categories of nonprofit organizations are not required to have their exemption recognized.)

Other Charity Law

As you may imagine, there is a lot more to charity law than the foregoing. These other laws apply to charities that are the subject of your gifts, to charities that philanthropists establish, and charities that receive grants from charities they form.

Here are the basics:

- *Private Inurement Doctrine.* Tax-exempt charities are subject to the law that states that their net earnings may not inure to the private benefit of related persons. These persons are known as *insiders.* They include trustees, directors, officers, their family members, and businesses and other entities they control. Unreasonable transactions and other arrangements, such as excessive compensation and unwarranted use of facilities, between a charitable organization and an insider can lead to loss of tax exemption.

- *Private Benefit Doctrine.* The private benefit doctrine, applicable to all charities, is much alike in scope with the private inurement doctrine. The principal differences between the two doctrines are that private benefit can occur with anyone (an insider is not required) and the law tolerates incidental private benefit. Unreasonable transactions and other arrangements between a charitable organization and a person in his, her, or its private capacity can lead to loss of tax exemption.

- *Attempts to Influence Legislation.* An exempt charitable organization is not supposed to engage in the dissemination of propaganda or other types of substantial attempts to influence legislation. Violation of this rule can lead to penalty taxes and/or loss of tax exemption. (See Chapter 5)

- *Political Campaign Activities.* Exempt charitable organizations are forbidden from participating or intervening in a campaign for or in opposition to a candidate for public office. (This may be the most violated rule in the Internal Revenue Code.) Violation of this rule can lead to penalty taxes and/or loss of tax exemption.

- *Public Policy Doctrine.* Exempt charitable organizations may not engage in any activities that are contrary to federal public policy. This is not statutory law or law found in the tax regulations but law grafted onto those two bodies of law by the Supreme Court. In the principal case, which held that discrimination on the basis of race by tax-exempt schools is a violation of established federal public policy, the Court sweepingly wrote that "[h]istory buttresses logic to make clear that, to warrant [tax] exemption [as a charitable entity] an institution must...demonstrably serve and be in harmony with the public interest" and not have a purpose that is "so at odds with the common community conscience as to undermine any public benefit that might otherwise be conferred." This doctrine raises questions, such as what exactly is federal public policy and who determines it. The answer to the latter question is that it is the IRS that initially makes the determination and the Supreme Court that ultimately does so. This Court opinion was issued in 1983; there have not been many subsequent applications of the public policy doctrine. Yet, charitable organizations should always operate with this doctrine in mind. Violation of this rule can lead to loss of tax exemption and eligibility for deductible charitable gifts.

- *Commerciality Doctrine.* Tax-exempt charitable organizations will lose or be denied exempt status if they are operated in a commercial manner. This is another body of law invented by the judiciary. This doctrine, however, is a nonsensical disaster. On its face, it appears to make sense: An entity ought not be an exempt charitable organization if it operates just like a for-profit business, thereby operating in competition with these businesses. The problem, however, lies in the criteria for determining commerciality that the courts have conjured; they are completely unrealistic and in some instances wrong as a matter of law. The criteria include selling goods or services for fees, engaging in marketing activities, and not receiving charitable gifts or grants. Of course, public charities sell goods and services for fee revenue all the time; examples are hospitals, schools, and theaters. Many charitable organizations engage in advertising and other forms of marketing. Also, as the rules for service provider publicly supported charities (see Chapter 5) illustrate, an entity can be charitable without receiving gifts or grants. But charities need to be careful with the commerciality doctrine; violations of this law can lead to loss of tax exemption.

- *Unrelated Business.* Exempt charities can engage in activities that are not related to their exempt purpose, as long as these activities are not substantial. Income tax must be paid on net unrelated business income. Various exceptions are embedded in this body of law. (See Chapter 6)

- *Fundraising Regulation.* Charitable organizations that engage in fundraising are subject to regulation by nearly every state. This regulation includes a registration (licensing) process and annual reporting. Civil and criminal penalties may apply if these charitable solicitation laws are violated. (See Chapter 5)
- *Subsidiaries.* Tax-exempt charities generally can have for-profit or tax-exempt subsidiaries. Caution must be exercised here by keeping these entities legally distinct, unless both parent and subsidiary are charitable entities. This aspect of the matter is particularly critical in the case of for-profit subsidiaries. The activities of a subsidiary can be attributed to the charitable parent (usually a very bad outcome) for tax law purposes. This type of attribution can occur when the parent charity is involved, on a day-to-day basis, in the management of the subsidiary or the subsidiary is perceived as an extension or instrumentality of the parent. Attribution of a subsidiary's functions to a charity can lead to loss of exemption. Private foundations essentially cannot utilize for-profit subsidiaries because of application of the excess business holdings rules (see Chapter 3).
- *Joint Ventures.* Tax-exempt charities may participate in partnerships and other forms of joint ventures. Problems can arise, however, where other venturers are noncharitable organizations; matters are more acute if they are for-profit entities. Here, the difficulty is that the activities of the persons in the venture are attributed to each other, frequently causing forms of private benefit. Arrangements that give rise to unwarranted private benefit can, as noted, lead to loss of exemption.
- *Annual Reporting.* With some exceptions (most notably for certain religious organizations), exempt charitable organizations (and other types of exempt entities) must annually file information returns with the IRS. The filing requirement generally depends on the organizations' financial size and, in some instances, what they do. A major dividing line is this: Generally, IRS Form 990 must be filed by exempt organizations that have either gross receipts greater than or equal to $200,000 or total assets greater than or equal to $500,000 at the end of their tax year. Generally, if an exempt organization has gross receipts less than $200,000 and total assets at year-end less than $500,000, it can file a simpler annual information return—Form 990-EZ. Nonetheless, four types of organizations must file Form 990 irrespective of their financial characteristics: (1) sponsoring organizations of

donor-advised funds (see Chapter 4), (2) organizations that operate one or more hospital facilities (see Chapter 5), (3) nonprofit health insurance issuers, and (4) certain parent organizations controlling subsidiaries. Supporting organizations (see Chapter 5) must (except for certain religious ones) file Form 990 or 990-EZ. Irrespective of the foregoing, private foundations file Form 990-PF. Organizations reporting unrelated business income file a form of tax return, Form 990-T.

- *Disclosure Rules.* Generally, the applications for recognition of tax exemption, where a favorable determination letter is issued, must be made public, including related correspondence and other documents. The most recent three years of annual information returns of exempt organizations must be disclosed. The unrelated business income tax return filed by exempt charitable organizations is also a public document.

- *Private Foundations.* As explained in the next chapter, some of the foregoing law topics are more stringent in the case of private foundations. Particularly notable in this regard are the rules concerning legislative and political campaign activities, and the laws pertaining to the conduct of unrelated business.

Chapter 3

Private Foundations

The most common type of charitable organization formed by philanthropists in the U.S. is the private foundation. The explanations for this sweeping statement appears at the end of this chapter. First, however, attention need to be given to what a private foundation is and does.

What is a *Private Foundation*?
Clients frequently ask: "What is a private foundation?" They usually add, "We've heard the term, but what exactly does it mean?" They are usually thinking of the Bill and Melinda Gates Foundation which, as the largest charity in the universe, does not usefully serve as a helpful model.

The first thought that always comes to my mind, on hearing these questions, is to respond by parroting what the statute (the Internal Revenue Code) says. In this instance, that type of response would not be of much use. (This is why statute-reading is best left to lawyers, not clients.) Here is what that form of response would be: "A private foundation is a tax-exempt charitable organization that is not a public charity." Needless to say, that answer would produce only a blank stare.

So, instead I offer my generic definition of the term *private foundation*. It is not found in any statute or tax regulation but is my distillation of what the two words mean. A typical private foundation has five characteristics:

- It is a tax-exempt charitable organization. (See Chapter 2)

- It is funded from one source. That source may be an individual, a married or unmarried couple, siblings, a family, or a for-profit business.
- It is funded on one occasion. The occasion may be a day in the life of a donor or donors or at the death of a donor. The latter approach has the private foundation created out of a decedent's estate.
- Its ongoing revenue is derived from investment income arising from the initial gift. Additional contributions may be made to a private foundation, but that is rare.
- It makes grants for charitable purposes as its program activity.

Thus, to revisit the circumstances of Carl and Nancy Jones, they could establish the Carl and Nancy Jones Foundation. Or, if Robert and Priscilla are involved, the Carl and Nancy Jones Foundation, or simply the Jones Family Foundation, could be formed. The foundation could be funded with the entire $100 million. That sum of money would be invested, say at a 5 percent return, giving the foundation annual revenue of $5 million (not taking into account any appreciation in the value of investment property). Grants and operating expenses would be paid out of that annual revenue flow.

Disqualified Persons

At the close of Chapter 2, reference was made to the private inurement doctrine and the fact that that body of law concerns transactions and other arrangements with a charity's insiders. In the parlance of private foundation law, insiders are known as *disqualified persons*. (Admittedly, this is not the most welcoming of terms.) As will be seen, it is important that every private foundation understand who its disqualified persons are.

There are seven principal categories of disqualified persons:

- *The founder or founders of a private foundation.* The technical term for the founder of a private foundation is *substantial contributor.* Generally, a substantial contributor is a person who contributed or bequeathed an aggregate amount of more than the higher of (1) 2 percent of the total contributions and bequests received by the private foundation before the close of its tax year in which the contribution or bequest is received by the foundation from that person or (2) $5,000. Since those thresholds (not changed since their enactment in 1969) are ridiculously low, it is literally impossible for a foundation funder of any consequence to escape substantial contributor status and thus disqualified person status. A person can be a substantial contributor to a private foundation and not be one of its founders, but that rarely happens. In the case of a trust, the creator of it is always a substantial contributor.

- *The private foundation's managers.* There are five ways to be a foundation manager. Three are obvious: the foundation's trustees, directors, and officers. The fourth way to be a foundation manager is to be an individual having powers or responsibilities that are similar to the foundation's trustees, directors, and officers. (This means that an individual can't escape disqualified person status simply by avoiding labels of positions.) The fifth way to be a foundation manager is to be an employee of a foundation who, with respect to any act or failure to act, has authority or responsibility with respect to the act or failure to act.
- *20-percent owners.* An owner of more than 20 percent of an entity that is a substantial contributor to the foundation is a disqualified person. Thus, this type of disqualified person is an owner of more than 20 percent of the total combined voting power of a corporation, the profits interest of a partnership, or the beneficial interest of a trust or unincorporated enterprise, where one of those entities is a substantial contributor to the foundation.
- *Family members.* An individual is a disqualified person with respect to a private foundation if the individual is a member of the family of an individual referenced in the foregoing three categories. The *family* of an individual is the individual's spouse, ancestors, children, grandchildren, greatgrandchildren, and the spouses of children, grandchildren, and greatgrandchildren. Note that an individual's brothers and sisters are not encompassed by this definition.
- *35-percent controlled corporations.* A corporation is a disqualified person with respect to a private foundation if one or more persons referenced in the foregoing four categories own more than 35 percent of the total combined voting power of the entity.
- *35-percent controlled partnerships.* A partnership is a disqualified person with respect to a private foundation if one or more persons referenced in the first four of the foregoing categories own more than 35 percent of the profits interest in the entity.
- *35-percent controlled trust or estate.* A trust or estate is a disqualified person with respect to a private foundation if one or more persons referenced in

the first four of the foregoing categories own more than 35 percent of the beneficial interest in the entity.

There are two other ways a person can be disqualified. One way is to be another private foundation that is controlled by those who control the foundation involved or is substantially funded by the same persons who funded the foundation involved; this definition of disqualified person is used only in connection with the excess business holdings rules (see below). The second of these ways is to be a government official (as opposed to being a mere government employee); this definition of disqualified person is used only in connection with the self-dealing rules (see below).

For private foundations that have been in existence for a significant period of time and/or have a large governing board, the matter of keeping track of who or what is a disqualified person with respect to the foundation can be tricky, comparable to tracing within an elaborate ancestral tree. Individuals are born, die, become married, become divorced, and/or become adopted on an ongoing basis. Persons' ownership interests in an entity can be acquired or disposed of; ownership percentages can fluctuate. A person with respect to a private foundation should be tasked with the job of maintaining an up-to-date list of its disqualified persons.

Governance of Foundations

Private foundations generally have governing boards. If the foundation is structured as a trust, it can have only one trustee (an individual or an institution such as a bank). Otherwise, state law is likely to require that the foundation's board consist of at least three individuals, who are at least 18 years of age. These individuals can include the founders of the foundation, their family members, or anyone else that those individuals may wish to have on the board. Those forming a foundation may wish to keep nonfamily members in the minority, so that the founders and their family have control of the foundation.

These other board members can be friends, professional colleagues, the foundation's lawyer, the foundation's accountant, and the like. (Personally, I will not sit on client's boards, whether they are private foundations or other types of nonprofit organizations. One, it is a conflict of interest, albeit a lawful one. Two, I have tried it and sometimes found it difficult to separate board work from lawyer's work. Three, I am a little leery of the potential for personal liability.)

Thus, for example, if Carl and Nancy Jones establish a private foundation, both of them can serve on the foundation's board. If their parents wish it, Carl and/or

Priscilla can also be on the board. If they want a larger board or a board with an odd number of individuals (as opposed to odd individuals), friends, neighbors, or colleagues can be included.

What do Foundations Do?

As noted, the typical (or "standard") private foundation is a maker of grants for charitable purposes. (See the discussion of private operating foundations next.) The founders of the foundation, or perhaps the governing board, will decide what the foundation's funding interests and priorities are. (The smorgasbord is described in Chapter 2.) Once those are determined, the foundation may wish to develop a brochure and/or a website summarizing its area(s) of funding. The foundation may want to develop a prototype grant application. The foundation is not required by law to do this; it may adopt a policy that it will not entertain unsolicited grant requests.

As also noted, the private foundation's grants must be for charitable *purposes*. The grants do not necessarily have to be to charitable *organizations*. Most private foundations confine their grantees to public charities. (See Chapter 5.) Others will make grants to individuals and/or to noncharitable organizations, including for-profit entities. (More on this below.) These are policy decisions to be resolved by the foundation's founders or overall management.

A private foundation may have one or more employees. (Yes, under most circumstances, individuals who are disqualified persons can be employees of the foundation.) A common type of foundation employee is the grant request reviewer, who will decide what grant requests to fund, the amount of the grants, whether site visits are required, and the like. Smaller foundations may decide to have all grants approved by the board.

Private foundations can have outside consultants, such as lawyers, accountants, and investment advisors and managers. Foundations can own property, whether used for investment or as part of program activity, such as an office building (or condominium). If so, a property manager may be involved.

Private Operating Foundations

A tax-exempt charitable organization can be a hybrid, a blend of private foundation and public charity features. An illustration of these hybrids is the private operating foundation, so named because, as the name indicates, it operates (and funds) its own programs, rather than make grants to others.

Typically, a private operating foundation is an endowed institution operating one or more charitable programs. A museum or a library, for example, may be structured as a private operating foundation. (These are types of entities that are not specifically identified in the law as public charities.) Thus, one of the decisions to be confronted by a foundation founder or perhaps a foundation board is whether to function as a standard grantmaking foundation or an operating foundation.

To be a private operating foundation, a private foundation must satisfy an *income test*, which requires that a specific amount be spent on directly conducted charitable programs, determined by either its actual income or a hypothetical minimum investment return. In addition, a private operating foundation must meet one of three other tests: an asset test, an endowment test, or a support test. The *asset test* requires that substantially all (i.e., at least 65 percent) of the foundation's assets be actively used in its programming. The *endowment test* is satisfied if the foundation normally expends its funds directly for the active conduct of its charitable activities in an amount equal to at least two-thirds of its minimum investment return. The *support test* is actually a clump of three requirements: (1) the foundation must receive substantially all (i.e., at least 85 percent) of its financial support from the public and from at least five tax-exempt organizations that are not disqualified persons with respect to it, (2) no more than 25 percent of that support can come from any one of these organizations, and (3) not more than 50 percent of the foundation's support can be in the form of investment income.

A private operating foundation is exempt from the excise tax on the failure to meet the mandatory distribution requirement imposed on standard private foundations (see below). This type of foundation is treated as a public charity for purposes of the percentage limitations that restrict the amount of charitable contributions individuals can annually deduct (see Chapter 7).

Private Foundation Rules

The various provisions of law that are lumped together as the *private foundation rules* collectively constitute the biggest disadvantage to private foundation status for a tax-exempt charitable organization. There are seven of these laws.

Each of these groups of laws involves one or more excise taxes. The first five of them are often referred to (incorrectly) as *prohibitions*. In fact, the Internal Revenue Code does not prohibit anything. There is no law that states, for example: "Thou shalt not engage in an act of self-dealing." It's just that the various taxes, coupled with the correction and reporting requirements (see below), are so onerous that the fear of becoming entangled in them amounts, as a practical matter, to a prohibition.

In some of these instances, taxes fall on private foundations and foundation managers (see above). There are initial (or first-tier) excise taxes and additional (or second-tier) excise taxes. One of the types of termination taxes is, in reality, an IRS confiscation of a foundation's income and assets.

Self-Dealing

Perhaps the most terrifying of the private foundation rules are the provisions concerning self-dealing. Here lies great complexity and quite a few traps. (In other words, this realm is a lawyer's delight.) Examined in this context are transactions and other arrangements, direct and indirect, between a private foundation and a disqualified person (see above) with respect to it.

Fifteen ways self-dealing can generally occur exist: (1) sale or exchange, or leasing, of property between a private foundation and a disqualified person; (2) lending of money or other extension of credit between a private foundation and a disqualified person; (3) furnishing of goods, services, or facilities between a private foundation and a disqualified person; (4) payment of compensation, or payment or reimbursement of expenses, by a private foundation to a disqualified person; (5) transfer to, or use by or for the benefit of, a disqualified person of the income or assets of a private foundation; and (6) the agreement by a private foundation to make a payment of money or other property to a government official.

There are several exceptions to these general rules. One is that the lending of money by a disqualified person to a private foundation is not self-dealing if the loan is without interest or other charge and the proceeds of the loan are used exclusively for charitable purposes.

Another exception is that the furnishing of goods, services, or facilities by a disqualified person to a private foundation is not an act of self-dealing if the furnishing is without charge and the goods, services, and facilities furnished are used exclusively for charitable purposes. Likewise. the furnishing of goods, services, or facilities by a private foundation to a disqualified person is not self-dealing if the furnishing is made on a basis no more favorable than that on which the goods, services, or facilities are made available to the public.

The rules causing foundation compensation of a government official entail a variety of exceptions, such as the paying of certain prizes and awards, the granting of certain scholarships or fellowships, payments from a pension or profit-sharing plan, and the payment of certain annuities.

The exception from the self-dealing rules that generally is the most important is the *personal services* exception. It is this exception that allows private foundations to compensate individuals, who are disqualified persons, as employees or independent contractors. This exception applies where the payment of compensation (and the payment or reimbursement of expenses) by a private foundation to a disqualified person (other than a government official) is for personal services that are reasonable and necessary to carrying out the exempt purposes of the foundation, assuming the compensation (or payment or reimbursement) is not excessive.

The term *personal services* is defined by the IRS to mean services that are professional or managerial in nature. Thus, grant administrators can be compensated even if they are disqualified persons, as can board members of a foundation (assuming the amounts are not excessive). Also, professionals such as lawyers, accountants, and investment advisors and managers can be paid pursuant to this exception. By contrast, secretarial and brokerage services do not qualify.

The facts of a court case illustrate how draconian the self-dealing rules can be. A private foundation had recently acquired an office building as its headquarters. The foundation's board of directors was deciding on the hiring of a janitorial services company to regularly clean the building. It so happened that one of the foundation's directors wholly owned such a company. The director offered the services of his company to the foundation at one-half the market rate for such services. The board thought that was a good deal for the foundation; it immediately accepted the offer. An IRS examination of the foundation thereafter ensued; the agent charged the private foundation with self-dealing because it purchased services from the janitorial company, which was a disqualified person with respect to the foundation. The foundation vehemently protested, arguing that the cleaning services were obviously reasonable and necessary for the conduct of exempt activities and the charge for the services was obviously not excessive. The IRS agent agreed with the foundation on those two points but asserted that the janitorial services were not personal services. The matter went to court, where the IRS prevailed. Janitorial services are not, the judge ruled, professional or managerial in nature. The fact that the private foundation received a good deal on the services was irrelevant.

The excise tax on an act of self-dealing is 10 percent of the amount involved. This tax is paid by the self-dealing disqualified person (other than a foundation manager). If this tax is imposed, an excise tax is imposed on the participation by a foundation manager in the act, if the manager knew it was self-dealing, unless the participation in the act was not willful and was due to reasonable cause.

If that initial tax is imposed and the self-dealing act is not timely corrected, another excise tax is imposed on the private foundation; that tax is 200 percent of the amount involved. If that additional tax is imposed and if a foundation manager refused to agree to part or all of the correction, an excise tax in the amount of 50 percent of the amount involved is imposed on the manager.

If it is any solace, the additional taxes imposed on foundation managers are capped, as to an act of self-dealing, at $20,000. But if more than one person is liable for self-dealing taxes, all of them are jointly and severally liable for the taxes. The IRS lacks the ability to abate the self-dealing taxes.

The term *correction*, in this context, means, with respect to an act of self-dealing, "undoing the transaction to the extent possible, but in any case placing the private foundation in a financial position not worse than that in which it would be if the disqualified person were dealing under the highest fiduciary standards."

Mandatory Payout

Private foundations are subject to a mandatory payout rule. The amount that must be paid out, with respect to each year, is an amount equal to 5 percent of the value of the foundation's noncharitable (investment) assets. This means that foundation management must decide which assets are being held for investment purposes and which assets are being used in achievement of the foundation's exempt purposes. The 5 percent payout amount is known as the *minimum investment return*.

The amounts that must be paid out are termed *qualifying distributions*. The payments may be for grants and other expenses necessary to accomplish exempt purposes. A private foundation may fund a specific project over a multi-year period; if it wishes, it can obtain a payout credit at the outset for this *set-aside* arrangement. Generally, a grant is not considered a qualifying distribution if paid to (1) an organization that is controlled, directly or indirectly, by the foundation or one or more disqualified persons with respect to it, or (2) a nonfunctionally integrated Type III supporting organization (see Chapter 5).

A private foundation has the year of the payout calculation and the immediately subsequent year to make the payout as determined in the calculation year. Despite this somewhat alleviating rule, the mandatory payout requirement generally forces private foundations to invest in such a way as to generate income in an amount to meet the payout obligation. If that investment income amount is insufficient, the foundation must, to avoid penalty taxes, dip into its principal to make up the difference.

An excise tax of 30 percent is imposed on the amount of a private foundation's income that should have been timely distributed but was not. If this matter has not been rectified by the close of the *taxable period* involved, an additional tax is imposed on the undistributed income at the rate of 100 percent. The IRS has the authority to abate these taxes.

Excess Business Holdings

Private foundations are restricted as to the extent of their holdings in business enterprises, such as corporations and partnerships. The federal tax law differentiates between permitted holdings and impermissible (or excess) holdings.

The general rule is that a private foundation cannot, without incurring penalty taxes, have more than a 20-percent interest in a business enterprise. Holdings by disqualified persons with respect to the foundation are taken into account in determining this percentage. If it can be shown that one or more third parties have control of the enterprise, the allowable percentage rises to 35. Foundations' holdings of 2 percent or less in business enterprises are disregarded for these purposes.

A private foundation may acquire a business enterprise by gift or bequest. If that happens, the foundation has five years to dispose of holdings that are excess holdings. Moreover, in the case of "unusually large" gifts of "diverse holdings" or holdings with "complex corporate structures," the IRS has the discretion to allow another five-year disposition period if diligent efforts to dispose the excess holdings have been made and a plan is in place to effectuate the disposition before the close of the extended period.

The term *business enterprise* does not include a *functionally related business*. This type of business (1) is a trade or business that is not an unrelated business (see Chapter 6) or (2), in the parlance of the statute, is "an activity which is carried on within a larger aggregate of similar activities or within a larger complex of other endeavors which is related (aside from the need of the organization for income or funds or the use it makes of the profits derived) to the exempt purposes of the organization." Also, a functionally related business does not include a trade or business at least 95 percent of the gross income of which is derived from passive sources.

A private foundation is subject to an excise tax of 10 percent on the value of any excess business holdings. If, after the close of the *taxable period*, excess holdings remain, the foundation is hit with an additional excise tax equal to 200 percent of the holdings. The IRS has the authority to abate these taxes.

Jeopardizing Investments

Private foundations are expected to act prudently in investing their assets. Risky investments are to be avoided; these are termed investments that "jeopardize the carrying out of any of [the foundation's] exempt purposes" or *jeopardizing investments*, for short. There are no investments that are automatically considered jeopardizing investments.

These rules do not apply to *program-related investments*, which are investments, the primary purpose of which is to accomplish one or more charitable purposes and no significant purpose of which is the production of income or the appreciation of property. In most instances, the jeopardizing investments prohibition also does not apply to *mission-related investing*, where the foundation avoids investing in businesses it deems antithetical to its charitable mission, even though the investment practices generates a somewhat lesser financial return.

A private foundation that makes a jeopardizing investment is subject to an excise tax of 10 percent of the amount of the investment. If this tax is imposed, there is imposed on the participation of a foundation manager in the making of the investment, knowing that it is a jeopardizing investment, a tax equal to 10 percent of the amount of the investment, unless the participation is not willful and is due to reasonable cause.

If this initial tax is imposed on a private foundation and the investment is not timely removed from jeopardy (see below), an additional tax of 25 percent of the amount of the investment is imposed on the foundation. Where this additional tax is imposed, and a foundation manager refuses to agree to part or all of the removal from jeopardy, an excise tax of 5 percent of the amount of the investment is imposed on the manager.

The IRS has the authority to abate these taxes.

The maximum amount of the initial excise tax imposed on a foundation manager, with respect to any one investment, is $10,000. The maximum amount of the additional tax imposed on a foundation manager is $20,000. Again, there is joint and several liability for these taxes.

A jeopardizing investment is considered to be *removed from jeopardy* when, in the language of the statute, the investment is "sold or otherwise disposed of, and the proceeds of such sale or other disposition are not" jeopardizing investments.

Taxable Expenditures

A transaction or practice that is not taxed (or taxable) by reason of the foregoing bodies of law may nonetheless be penalized if it involves a *taxable expenditure*. Seven types of taxable expenditures lurk: (1) the carrying on of propaganda, or otherwise attempting, to influence legislation; (2) influencing the outcome of a public election; (3) the carrying on of a voter registration drive; (4) the making of a grant to an individual for travel, study, or similar purpose; (5) the making of a grant to certain supporting organizations (see Chapter 5); (6) the making of a grant to an organization that is not an eligible public charity (*id.*); and (7) the making of an expenditure for a noncharitable purpose. It is because of this body of law that most private foundations confine their grantees to qualifying public charities.

For purposes of the first category of taxable expenditure, the expenditures are those for any attempt to influence legislation through (1) an attempt to affect the opinion of the public or a segment of the public (known as *indirect* or *grass-roots lobbying*) and (2) communications with a member or employee of a legislative body or with any other government official or employee who may participate in the formulation of the legislation (known as *direct lobbying*).

Four exceptions to the lobbying restrictions are available: (1) making available the results of nonpartisan analysis, study, or research (essentially, educational undertakings (see Chapter 2)); (2) examinations and discussions of broad social, economic, and similar problems, even if the problems are of the type with which government would be expected to deal ultimately; (3) the provision of technical advice or assistance to a governmental body or a committee or subcommittee, in response to a written request; and (4) appearances before or communications to a legislative body with respect to a possible decision of the body which might affect the foundation's existence, powers and duties, tax-exempt status, or deductibility of contributions to it (known informally as the *self-defense exception*).

With respect to the third category of taxable expenditure, an exception is available for nonpartisan activities of a tax-exempt charitable organization where (1) the activities are not confined to a specific election period; (2) the activities are carried on in at least five states; (3) substantially all of the organization's income is expended directly for its exempt purposes; (4) substantially all of the organization's support is received from exempt organizations, the public, and/or governmental units; (5) no more than 25 percent of this support is from any one exempt organization; (6) no more than 50 percent of the support is gross investment income; and (7) contributions to it for voter registration drives are not subject to conditions that they be used in specific states or other governmental units or that they be only used in a specific election period.

Notwithstanding the fourth category of taxable expenditure, a private foundation may make grants to individuals where it is awarded on an objective and nondiscriminatory basis pursuant to a procedure approved in advance by the IRS. Moreover, it must be demonstrated to the IRS that the grant constitutes a scholarship or fellowship grant to be used for study at an educational institution, the grant constitutes a qualified prize or award, or the purpose of the grant is to achieve a specific objective, produce a report or other similar product, or improve or enhance a literary, artistic, musical, scientific, teaching, or other similar capacity, skill, or talent of the grantee.

When a private foundation seeks advance approval of its individual grant program, it should be prepared to provide the IRS with its grant procedure, a grant application form, and a listing of the members of its grants committee. Again, it is important to emphasize that it is the overall grant procedure that requires advance IRS approval, not the grants themselves. But private foundation grants made for travel, study, or other similar purposes, without prior IRS approval as to the procedure, are taxable expenditures.

With respect to the sixth category of taxable expenditure, the private foundation grants to entities that are not qualified public charities are not taxable expenditures if the foundation grantor exercises expenditure responsibility over the grant. This means that the foundation is assuming the responsibility to exert all reasonable efforts and to establish adequate procedures to (1) see that the grant is spent solely for the purpose or purposes for which it was made, (2) obtain full and complete reports from the grantee on how the funds are spent, and (3) make full and complete reports with respect to the expenditures to the IRS.

An excise tax in the amount of 20 percent of the amount of the taxable expenditure is imposed on the private foundation. Another initial excise tax is imposed on the agreement of a foundation manager to the making of an expenditure, knowing that it is a taxable expenditure, in the amount of 5 percent, unless the agreement is not willful and is due to reasonable cause.

If this initial tax is imposed on a private foundation and the expenditure is not timely corrected, an additional excise tax in the amount of 100 percent of the expenditure is imposed on the foundation. In a situation where this additional tax is imposed, if a foundation manager refused to agree to part or all the correction, an additional tax is imposed on the manager equal to 50 percent of the amount of the taxable expenditure.

The IRS has the authority to abate these taxes.

There is a maximum limit of $10,000 on the additional tax imposed on a private foundation. As to the additional tax imposed on foundation managers, the maximum limit is $20,000. Once again, the taxes on persons for the making of taxable expenditures are the subject of joint and several liability.

Correction in this context means recovering part or all of the expenditure to the extent recovery is possible. Where full recovery is not possible, additional forms of corrective action are prescribed. Correction also can mean obtaining or making the requisite reports, whether from the grantee or to the IRS.

Tax on Investment Income

Nearly all private foundations that are exempt from federal income tax must annually pay an excise tax of two percent on their net investment income. Where a foundation distributes its income in an amount greatly in excess of its mandatory payout amount (see above), this tax rate is reduced to one percent. *Investment income* includes interest, dividends, rent, royalties, and capital gain.

Termination of Status

A tax-exempt charitable organization that is classified as a private foundation can terminate its private foundation status. This termination can be voluntary, with the foundation either distributing all its assets and income to one or more qualified public charities or operating as a public charity. (See Chapter 5) These is no tax associated with a voluntary termination of private foundation status.

A private foundation status termination can also be involuntary. This type of termination arises where there have been either willful repeated acts or failures to act, or a willful and flagrant act or failure to act, giving rise to liability for one or more of the private foundation penalty excise taxes. In this situation, there is a termination tax which can be confiscatory, that is, equal to the value of the net assets of the foundation.

A special termination procedure is available to alleviate the situation where family members involved with a private foundation are quarreling over the foundation's funding priorities and programs or, for that matter, other reasons (e.g., unfolding divorces). One foundation can be chopped into two, three, or more foundations, each controlled by a family member and operated independently.

Advantages and Disadvantages

As is the case with nearly everything in life, a particular position or situation presents advantages and disadvantages. This is certainly the case with respect to private foundation status.

Here are the advantages associated with private foundation status:

- *Advantage #1*: Those who form the foundation can control it. Even a small group of individuals, such as a family, can control and manage a private foundation. This control can be manifested by governing board and officer positions. This factor alone is the biggest reason why individuals decide to use the private foundation approach.
- *Advantage #2*: Board members, officers, and family members can also be employees of the private foundation. Because these individuals are disqualified persons, the services they provide must, to avoid self-dealing difficulties, be personal services. That outcome is relatively easy to achieve.
- *Advantage #3*: Private foundations have enormous flexibility with respect to grantmaking purposes and priorities. There usually is no larger board or independent board to deal with in this regard (and many others). They can change pursuits at will, as long as they stay within the bounds of what is charitable. (See Chapter 2)
- *Advantage #4*: Private foundations are not required to meet the myriad of tax law requirements that are imposed on forms of public charities, such as churches, hospitals, publicly supported charities, and schools.
- *Advantage #5*. Private foundations do not have to engage in fundraising (although they can if they wish). Thus, they can avoid the rigors of federal and state fundraising regulation.
- *Advantage #6*: The process of applying for recognition of tax exemption will often be simpler and easier in the case of private foundations. The IRS is amply familiar with these types of entities. As long as it is competently prepared, the application should sail through the IRS.
- *Advantage #7*: With a private foundation, there is less likelihood of entanglement in the law imposed by the private inurement and private benefit doctrines. The price for this immunity is, of course, compliance with the self-dealing rules.

Here are the disadvantages associated with private foundation status:

- *Disadvantage #1*: Generally, the charitable giving rules tilt against private foundations. This is, without doubt, the biggest disadvantage to private foundation status. The amount individuals can annually deduct for the making of charitable contributions is usually lower when the gifts are made to private foundations than to public charities, many types of property gifts give rise to deduction amounts that are confined to the basis in the property where the donee is a private foundation, and more. (See Chapter 7) Consequently, the decision as to which type of entity to create will turn on the control factor (see above) versus the charitable deduction factor. Some of this, however, can be alleviated by causing the foundation to function as a private operating foundation.
- *Disadvantage #2*: The organization must comply with the private foundation rules to steer clear of the penalty excise taxes, both on foundations and their managers. A cure, however, is available for this: retention of competent lawyers and accountants to guide the foundation and its board through the maze.
- *Disadvantage #3*: Smaller private foundations must file a more complex annual information return than their public charity counterparts. Private foundations are required to file annual returns no matter what the size of the foundation; this is IRS Form 990-PF. These returns are complicated, largely due to the intricacies of the private foundation rules. Larger public charities file their annual returns on Form 990. Medium-sized public charities have a simpler return—the Form 990-EZ.
- *Disadvantage #4*: Private foundations are more constrained than public charities in terms of the extent they can attempt to influence legislative processes, because of the taxable expenditure rule.
- *Disadvantage #5*: Private foundations cannot have active unrelated business activity because of the limitations imposed by the excess business holdings rules. (See above) This potentially deprives foundations of this type of funding. Private foundations, however, can have related businesses and forms of passive unrelated business income (see Chapter 6).
- *Disadvantage #6*: A private foundation cannot be an organization that maintains one or more donor-advised funds (see Chapter 4).

- *Disadvantage #7*: Private foundations cannot make political campaign expenditures.
- *Disadvantage #8*: Where a relatively small amount of money is involved, it may not be practical to establish a private foundation. Of course, the same can be said with respect to forming a public charity. Aggressive and successful investing can grow the principal within a charity, if that is an option. Another way to do that is by fundraising. Private foundations rarely engage in fundraising, as noted, but they can. If a foundation is successful at fundraising, it can convert itself to a publicly supported charity. (See above and Chapter 5)

Chapter 4
Donor-Advised Funds

In the right circumstances, a donor-advised fund is the perfect alterative to a private foundation, and it can be preferable to a public charity. These vehicles have been in existence for decades. Yet, they did not become the subject of statutory law until 2006. There are no tax regulations on the topic, not even in proposed form, so the formal law in this regard is skimpy.

What is a *Donor-Advised Fund***?**
The first thing to understand about a donor-advised fund is that it is not a legal entity, like a corporation or a trust. A private foundation or a public charity is a legal entity—not so with a donor-advised fund. A donor-advised fund is an account within a charitable entity.

Here are the basic characteristics of a donor-advised fund:

- It is a fund (or account) within a tax-exempt charitable organization.
- It is separately identified by reference to contributions of one or more donors.
- The exempt charitable organization qualifies as a sponsoring organization, and thus owns and controls the fund.
- The donor to a donor-advised fund, or the donor's advisor, has, or reasonably expects to have, what the law terms "advisory privileges" with respect to the distribution or investment of amounts held in the fund. A *donor advisor* is a person designated as such by a donor.

The law provides some exceptions to this definition. For example, funds that make distributions only to a single identified organization or governmental entity, and certain funds where a donor or donor advisor provides advice as to which individuals receive grants for travel, study, or other similar purposes, are not donor-advised funds. For this exception to be available, however, (1) the person's advisory privileges must be performed exclusively by that person in the person's capacity as a member of a committee, all of the members of which are appointed by the sponsoring organization; (2) no combination of these persons, or their related persons, can control, directly or indirectly, the committee; and (3) all grants from the fund are awarded on an objective and nondiscriminatory basis pursuant to a procedure approved in advance by board of directors of the sponsoring organization, where the procedure is designed to assure that the grants involved meet the requirements of the rules imposed on private foundations in connection with the making of grants to individuals.

Also, the IRS has the authority to exempt a fund from treatment as a donor-advised fund where (1) the fund is advised by a committee, that is not directly or indirectly controlled by the donor or any person appointed or designated by the donor, for the purpose of advising with respect to distributions from the fund (and any related parties), or (2) the fund benefits a single identified charitable purpose. The agency has done this once, announcing that certain employer-sponsored disaster relief assistance funds do not constitute donor-advised funds.

A *sponsoring organization* is a public charity (see Chapter 5), other than a governmental body, that maintains one or more donor-advised funds. Thus, a private foundation cannot be a sponsoring organization. A sponsoring organization may be an entity that maintain a few donor-advised funds, along with many other charitable programs, or an entity that maintains donor-advised funds as its sole function.

Most sponsoring organizations are donative-type publicly supported charities (see Chapter 5). Contributions targeted for particular donor-advised funds are contributions to the sponsoring organization. These gifts are, in whole or in part, forms of public support for the sponsoring organization.

In addition to the federal tax law requirements, sponsoring organizations will have various internal policies and practices. A sponsoring organization will have a procedure for verifying the tax-exempt and public charity status of the prospective grantees. Allowable gifts to its donor-advised funds will likely be confined to contributions of money and publicly traded (liquid) securities. Grantees will be limited to public charities; thus, for example, grants for charitable purposes will not be made to individuals.

Here is an illustration of use of a donor-advised fund. Annabelle Clark just inherited $50,000. Not needing the money for her day-to-day existence, Annabelle decides to give the money to charity. She is happy to have the resulting charitable deduction(s) but is reluctant to simply scatter the $50,000 over a handful of charities. After consulting her favorite nonprofit lawyer, Sam, she decides to create a donor-advised fund. Annabelle lives in the city of Clio. With Sam's help, Annabelle finds her way to the Clio Community Foundation, a public charity that, among a range of programs, maintains donor-advised funds.

Annabelle executes a donor-advised fund agreement with the Clio Community Foundation, creating the Annabelle Clark Charitable Fund. This agreement gives Annabelle the privilege of advising the Foundation, from time to time, as to the making of grants from the Fund and advising the Foundation as to investment of the Fund's assets. It also names Sam as the donor advisor. The Foundation owns the assets and income of the Fund, and controls it. Annabelle gives the Foundation a check for $50,000, which is deposited in the Annabelle Clark Charitable Fund.

What Do These Funds Do?

In reality, donor-advised funds don't do much. They are accounts, holding the assets the sponsoring organization has selected for them, taking into account any advice provided by the donor, and the investment income that is generated by the assets.

A donor-advised fund is a grantmaking vehicle. The sponsoring organization makes grants from the fund to various charitable organizations, again, after considering advice from the donor. Therefore, in several ways, a donor-advised fund functions much the same as a private foundation (see Chapter 3).

As is explained next, what a donor-advised fund cannot do, or is penalized if it does do, is serve as an employer for a donor, a donor advisor, or a party related to them. Most sponsoring organizations do not permit these types of employment arrangements in any event.

Six months after establishing the Annabelle Clark Charitable Fund, Annabelle contacts the Clio Community Foundation and requests that a grant in the amount of $1,000 be made to one of Annabelle's favorite charities, the Clio Environmental Protection Society. The Foundation duly considers this advice, then decides to make the grant. In due course, the Clio Community Foundation sends a check, showing the payor as the Annabelle Clark Charitable Fund, to the Clio Environmental Society. The Society records the grant as coming from the Fund.

During this six-month period, the Fund earned $750. Following this grant, the balance in the Fund's account is $49,750.

Concept of the *Contribution*

As a matter of law, a transfer of money or other eligible property to a donor-advised fund is a *contribution* by the transferor and is a transaction that is *complete*. From time to time, a question is raised as to whether a transfer of property to a donor-advised fund is a gift, or whether the transfer is incomplete, in that the donor, by reserving an ability to advise as to grantmaking and/or investing, has retained some form of "right" that precludes the transfer from being a completed gift.

It is obviously clear that there must be a contribution before there can be a charitable contribution. Integral to the concept of the charitable contribution deduction is the fundamental requirement that the payment of money or other property to a charitable organization be pursuant to a transaction that constitutes a gift. (For these purposes, the words *contribution* and *gift* mean the same.)

The federal tax regulations contain this definition: A *contribution* is a "voluntary transfer of money or property that is made with no expectation of procuring financial benefit commensurate with the amount of the transfer." This definition reflects the observation of the U.S. Supreme Court that a *gift* is a transfer motivated by "detached or disinterested generosity." Any condition by which the putative donor retains complete dominion and control over the transferred property makes the gift incomplete. An incomplete gift cannot give rise to a charitable contribution.

The Supreme Court also ruled, in the context of explaining the concept of a charitable gift, that a "payment of money [or transfer of other property] generally cannot constitute a charitable contribution if the contributor expects a substantial benefit in return." Subsequently, the Court wrote that an exchange having an "inherently reciprocal nature" is not a gift and thus cannot be a charitable gift where the recipient is a charity. Conversely, when a benefit to a donor arising out of a transfer to a charitable organization is incidental, the benefit will not defeat the charitable deduction.

Thus, a *charitable gift* can be defined as a voluntary transfer of money or other property to a charitable organization without actual or anticipated receipt by the donor of more than incidental economic considerations or benefits in return. The value inherent in any economic consideration or benefit received in return, other than an incidental one, should be subtracted from the value of the total gift amount to determine the value (if any) of the actual gift (the deductible portion).

In most situations, once a donor has made a gift to a charity, the gift item becomes the property of the charitable organization and the donor retains no or little authority over the use or expenditure of the funds. Then there is the matter of the *conditional gift*, which is a gift made subject to the occurrence of an event, either before (*condition precedent*) or after (*condition subsequent*) the transaction.

The IRS challenged the donor-advised fund technique in court—and lost by reason of a decision issued in 1987. The IRS attempted to deny tax-exempt status to a public charity maintaining donor-advised funds, contending that the entity (now known as a sponsoring organization) was merely an association of donors for which commercial services were being performed for fees, and that the entity was violating the prohibitions on private inurement and private benefit (see Chapter 2). The IRS asserted that this organization's "activities are all originated, funded, and controlled by small related groups, by single individuals, or by families" and that "these individual donors retain full control of the funds."

The court, however, found that donors to the organization "relinquish all ownership and custody of the donated funds or property" and that the organization is "free to accept or reject any suggestion or request made by a donor." Indeed, the court enthused that the "goal" of the organization "is to create an effective national network to respond to many worthy charitable needs at the local level which in many cases might go unmet" and that its activities "promote public policy and represent the very essence of charitable benevolence as envisioned by Congress in enacting" tax-exempt status for charitable organizations.

Thus, today it is clear as a matter of law that a contribution to a sponsoring organization for the purpose of establishing a donor-advised fund is a charitable contribution. The retention by a donor of the ability to advise as to investment of the property in the donor-advised fund and/or advise as to the making of grants from the fund is not a *right* or *condition* (or other restriction) imposed on the gift. In the parlance of the statutory law, all that is retained is a form of *privilege*.

Donor-Directed Funds

Beware the *donor-directed fund*. This type of fund involves an arrangement between a charitable organization and a donor by which the donor retains one or more *rights* as to the subsequent investment and/or disposition of the subject of the gift. Consequently, a donor-directed fund is not a donor-advised fund.

The distinction between these two types of funds lies in what the federal tax law terms a *prohibited material restriction*. The test as to these restrictions is whether the transferee of assets is prevented from freely and effectively employing the transferred assets or the income generated by them for charitable purposes. For example, if the transferor reserved the right to direct one or more public charities to which the transferee must distribute the transferred assets and/or income, that would be a prohibited material restriction. The same is true with respect to restrictions on the ability of the transferee to maintain or manage the assets in the fund and with respect to any other condition imposed on the transferee that prevents it from exercising ultimate control over the assets received by the transferor.

Donor-Advised Fund Rules

A distribution from a donor-advised fund will give rise to a penalty tax if it is to (1) an individual, (2) any other person for a noncharitable purpose, or (3) any other noncharitable person for a charitable purpose unless expenditure responsibility (see Chapter 4) is exercised with respect to the distribution. This tax, at the rate of 20 percent of the amount involved, is imposed on the sponsoring organization.

Another tax, of 5 percent, is imposed on the agreement of a fund manager to the making of a taxable distribution, where the manager knew that the distribution was a taxable one. The term *fund manager* embraces the sponsoring organization's trustees, directors, officers, and any individual having the powers or responsibilities similar to those of the organization's trustees, directors, or officers. The term also includes, with respect to an act or failure to act, the employees of the sponsoring organization having authority or responsibility with respect to the act or failure to act. This tax is confined to $10,000 per transaction (if that is any solace). This tax is also subject to a joint and several liability requirement.

Note that the tax on the fund manager is levied where the manager knew that the distribution in which the manager was involved was a taxable distribution. There are no regulations in the donor-advised fund context that define this concept of *knowing*. (As noted, in this setting, there aren't any regulations at all.) This term is, however, addressed in the private foundation regulations, offering useful guidance to fund managers in the interim.

For example, a foundation manager is considered to have agreed to a taxable expenditure (see Chapter 3), knowing that the expenditure was a taxable one, only if the manager (1) had actual knowledge of sufficient facts so that , based solely on those facts, the expenditure would be a taxable one; (2) was aware that the expenditure under these circumstances may violate the federal tax law governing taxable expenditures; and (3) negligently failed to make reasonable attempts to ascertain whether the expenditure was a taxable one, or the manager was in fact aware that the expenditure was taxable. While the term *knowing* does not mean "having reason to know," evidence tending to show that a foundation manager had reason to know of a particular fact or particular rule is relevant in determining whether the manager had actual knowledge of that fact or rule.

Here is another place where a good lawyer can save the day. If a foundation manager, after full disclosure of a factual situation to a lawyer, relies on the written advice of counsel expressed in a reasoned legal opinion that an expenditure is not a taxable one, although the expenditure is subsequently held to be a taxable one, the manager's agreement to the expenditure will ordinarily not be considered *knowing* and will ordinarily be considered due to reasonable cause. A written legal opinion is considered *reasoned* even if it reaches a conclusion that is subsequently determined to be incorrect as long as the opinion was addressed to the facts and applicable law. Not surprisingly, a written legal opinion is not a reasoned one if it merely recites the facts and expresses a conclusion.

A taxable distribution does not take place where the distribution from a donor-advised fund is to an eligible public charity, the fund's sponsoring organization, or another donor-advised fund. The public charity that is ineligible in this regard is the *disqualified supporting organization*, which is (1) a nonfunctionally integrated Type III supporting organization and (2) an organization that is a Type I and Type II supporting organization, and a functionally integrated Type III supporting organization, where (a) the donor or any person designated by the donor for the purpose of advising with respect to distributions from a donor-advised fund and any related parties controls a supported organization of the organization or (b) the IRS has determined that a distribution to the organization is otherwise inappropriate. (These types of supporting organizations are discussed in Chapter 5.)

If a donor, donor advisor, or a person related to a donor or donor advisor with respect to a donor-advised fund provides advice as to a distribution from the fund that results in any of these persons receiving, directly or indirectly, a benefit that is more than incidental, an excise tax equal to 125 percent of the amount of the benefit is imposed on the person who advised as to the distribution and on the recipient of the benefit.

Also, if a manager of the sponsoring organization agreed to the making of the distribution, knowing that the distribution would confer more than an incidental benefit on a donor, donor advisor, or related person, the manager is subject to an excise tax equal to 10 percent of the amount involved. These taxes are subject to a joint and several liability requirement.

A grant, loan, payment of compensation, or other similar payment (such as reimbursement of expenses) from a donor-advised fund to a person that, with respect to the fund, is a donor, donor advisor, or a person related to a donor or donor advisor automatically is treated as an excess benefit transaction. Pursuant to the *excess benefit transaction* rules, also known as *intermediate sanctions*, a disqualified person receiving an excess benefit from a public charity (see Chapter 5) is subject to an excise tax of 25 percent of the excess amount. This rule in the donor-advised fund context means that the entire amount paid from the fund to any of these persons is a taxable excess benefit. Donors, donor advisors, and their related persons with respect to a donor-advised fund are *disqualified persons* (see Chapter 3) for intermediate sanctions law purposes with respect to transactions with the donor-advised fund, although not necessarily with respect to transactions with the sponsoring organization.

Annabelle Clark just inherited more money—this time, $5 million. Without consulting Sam (or any other competent nonprofit lawyer, Annabelle adds that sum to the Annabelle Clark Charitable Fund. Let's now assume that the Clio Community Foundation allows donors to pay themselves as employees of their donor-advised funds. Annabelle, overwhelmed by the amount of time she is now spending on grantmaking, again without consulting legal counsel, decides she is entitled to an annual salary of $100,000 from the Fund. She does this for three years, when the IRS, examining the Foundation, discovers this compensatory arrangement. Annabelle is assessed excise taxes in the amount of $75,000 ($300,000 × 25 percent), plus is required to correct this misstep by returning the $300,000 to the Fund, along with suitable interest (that is, *correcting* compensation transactions). Thus, this was a costly mistake for Annabelle. This rule is more stringent than the one for comparable transactions in the private foundation context.

The private foundation excess business holdings rules (see Chapter 3) apply to donor-advised funds. For this purpose, the term *disqualified person* means, with respect to a donor-advised fund, a donor, donor-advisor, member of the family of either of these persons, and a 35-percent-controlled entity of any of the foregoing persons. This rule of law does not have much impact because sponsoring organizations typically will not accept contributions of business enterprises.

Contributions to a sponsoring organization for maintenance in one or more donor-advised fund are not eligible for a charitable deduction for federal income tax purposes if the sponsoring organization is a fraternal society, a cemetery company, or a veterans' organization (all charitable organizations for charitable giving purposes generally). Contributions to a sponsoring organization for maintenance in one or more funds are not eligible for a charitable deduction for federal estate or gift tax purposes if the sponsoring organization is a fraternal society or a veterans' organization. Contributions to a sponsoring organization for maintenance in one or more funds are ineligible for a charitable deduction for income, estate, or gift tax purposes if the sponsoring organization is a nonfunctionally integrated Type III supporting organization.

A donor must obtain, with respect to each charitable contribution to a sponsoring organization to be maintained in a donor-advised fund, a contemporaneous written acknowledgement from the organization that the organization has exclusive legal control over the funds or assets contributed. (This fact should be reflected in the donor-advised fund agreement.) This requirement is in addition to the other charitable gift substantiation requirements (see Chapter 7).

A sponsoring organization is required to disclose on its annual information return the number of donor-advised funds it maintains, the aggregate value of the assets held in the funds as of the close of the organization's tax year, and the aggregate contributions to and grants from these funds during the year. When seeking recognition of tax-exempt status (see Chapter 2), a sponsoring organization must disclose whether it intends to maintain donor-advised funds. As to this latter rule, the organization must provide information regarding its planned operation of these funds, including a description of the procedures it intends to use to (1) communicate to donors and donor advisors that assets held in the funds are the property of the sponsoring organization and (2) ensure that distributions from donor-advised funds do not result in more than an incidental benefit to any person.

Pending Controversies
Those contemplating use of donor-advised funds should be aware of this pending controversy: Whether donor-advised funds should be subject to a mandatory payout, such as the scheme applicable to private foundations (see Chapter 3).

Before addressing that issue, it is helpful to look at the world of donor-advised funds from a statistical viewpoint. The first study of these funds following enactment of the statutory rules was conducted by the Department of the Treasury; this report, based on statistics for 2006, was issued late in 2011. The report observed that donor-advised funds "play an important role in the charitable sector" and "have been a helpful development for donors in the charitable sector."

Sponsoring organizations received $59.5 billion in 2006, including $9 billion in contributions to donor-advised funds. These organizations had total expenses of $37.7 billion, including $5.7 billion in grants paid from donor-advised funds, $6.8

billion in other grants, and $20.7 billion in program outlays. These organizations had a net worth of $211.3 billion as of the close of the year. The 2,398 sponsoring organizations maintaining donor-advised funds owned 160,000 of them, entailing assets valued at $31.1 billion as of the end of the year.

This report references sponsoring organizations that have a "national reach" and have as their primary role services as "intermediaries between donors and a broad range of charities providing direct charitable services by sponsoring and maintaining donor-advised funds and other similar charitable funds." These organizations are referred to by the Treasury as *national donor-advised funds*. A subset of national donor-advised funds is funds that are sponsored by charities affiliated by financial institutions—accorded the most unfortunate name of *commercial national donor-advised funds*.

Commercial national donor-advised funds had, in the aggregate, an average of $424.5 million in total assets and median assets of $58.9 million. The average payout rate for all donor-advised funds in 2006 was 9.3 percent. For the commercial national donor-advised funds, the average payout rate was 14.2 percent. These numbers led the Treasury to conclude that it would be "premature to recommend a distribution requirement for [donor-advised funds] at this point."

The only other comprehensive study of donor-advised funds by the federal government was issued by the Congressional Research Service in mid-2012, based on data for 2008. In that year, more than 181,000 donor-advised fund accounts were maintained. About 1,800 organizations maintained at least one donor-advised fund.

The CRS report stated that a small percentage of sponsoring organizations held a large number of donor-advised funds. Fifty-one organizations (about 3 percent of all sponsoring organizations) had 500 or more funds. More than 121,000 of all funds (or two-thirds of them) were maintained by organizations that have at least 500 donor-advised funds. For the year, sponsoring organizations held $29.5 billion in donor-advised fund assets. On average, assets per donor-advised fund had a value of about $162,000. Nearly all donor-advised funds (87 percent) were held by sponsoring organization that maintained 100 or more of these funds. Total contributions to donor-advised funds amounted to $7.1 billion. These contributions represented approximately 3.3 percent of total individual giving. The average contribution per fund was $39,103.

Sponsoring organizations paid out about $7 billion in grants. On average, $38,641 in grants were paid per donor-advised fund. Out of the 1,828 sponsoring organizations included in the sample, 453 did not make any grants. The organizations that sponsored donor-advised funds but did not pay grants held $280.4 billion in assets in 2008.

The average payout rate across sponsoring organizations was 13.1 percent. The median payout rate was 6.1 percent; this rate was said by the CRS to be "skewed" by the payout rates of organizations with "unusually large payout" (well, of course). Forty-three percent of sponsoring organizations had an average payout rate of less than 5 percent. Twenty-six percent of these organizations did not have any payouts.

This study included a review of 21 "commercial" sponsoring organizations maintaining donor-advised funds in 2008. In that year, 46.7 percent of these funds were maintained by these organizations. For that year, 34.3 percent of donor-advised funds' assets, 39.2 percent of funds' contributions, and 39.7 percent of funds' grants involved "commercial" sponsoring organizations. The average payout rate for "commercial" donor-advised funds was 26.5 percent.

The CRS report, which has an anti-donor-advised fund tone, observed that, since "commercial" sponsoring organizations "tend to sponsor a large number of individual accounts (2,720 on average), it is possible that there is substantial variation in payout rates across individual accounts that is masked by the aggregate nature of available data." This clunky sentence tells me that it is quite obvious that there is "substantial variation in [these] payout rates."

Unlike the Treasury, which found discussion of a donor-advised fund mandatory payout "premature," the CRS jumped right into the fray. It wrote that "there is ample reason to reject the notion that an aggregate payout ratio higher than that of private foundations provides a good rationale for not imposing such requirements on a per account basis." The CRS report recalled that the Treasury report rejected application of the private foundation rules (see Chapter 3) to donor-advised funds on the ground that control of the funds is in the sponsoring organizations which are public charities (see Chapter 5). The CRS report rejected this most accurate observation, stating that—in complete ignorance of the applicable law—"donors [to advised funds] appear to have actual control of grant-making [from them] because sponsoring organizations typically follow their advice." That, my friends, is absurd!

The CRS report concluded with this: "In some ways, the fundamental policy issue about how freely to allow donors to make contributions that are not immediately used for charitable purposes [including supporting organizations (see Chapter 5)] is whether such arrangements increase charitable giving per dollar of cost or decrease it. Allowing for contributions to accumulate and earn a tax-free return [see Chapter 7] increases the benefit to the donor and thus may increase contributions to funds or foundations, albeit it at an additional cost. Such arrangements can also reduce current charitable giving by encouraging fund accumulation, a concern that presumably motivated the minimum distribution rules for private foundations. [Donor-advised funds] differ from foundations in some ways, including the legal technicalities, but in practice, are very similar. One concern that remains for both [private] foundations and [donor-advised funds] is how soon donations are put to charitable use."

Two articles in the November 6, 2014, issue of the *Chronicle of Philanthropy* offer a useful juxtaposition of views. One article was written by Ken Nopar, who advises charitable organizations on how they can work more effectively with wealth and legal advisors to donors. Nopar rejects the view that donor-advised funds largely serve the function of enabling the wealthy to park their contributions and still receive tax deductions, and divert gifts from charities with needed programs. He believes that these funds make it easier for lawyers and similar advisors to "talk to their clients about philanthropy," which leads to more giving. He notes that grants from donor-advised funds are typically larger than contributions directly by individuals. He asserts that "very few" donor-advised funds fail to make grants and that "often" sponsoring organizations contact account holders to encourage grantmaking, stating that "on average, 16 percent is granted every year" from donor-advised funds. Nopar encourages charities to regard these funds as "friends," writing that donor-advised funds are "established by donors at many levels of wealth for multiple reasons [see below], including their desire to distribute more of their assets to charities and less in taxes to the government."

Then there is Alan Cantor, billed as a fundraising consultant, who asserts that "money is flowing into advised funds, rather than to nonprofits that provide actual services." Indeed, Cantor believes that the existence of donor-advised funds is evidence of an "inexorable takeover of the charitable sector by Wall Street." (No hyperbole there!) Donors are to these funds are said to have "de facto control" over distributions from the fund (not true) "without the hassle and expense of creating a private foundation" (somewhat true). Cantor sees the world of charitable giving as "largely a zero-fund game." (This is not true; charitable giving increases almost annually, even when adjusted for the rate of inflation.) Thus, he writes that "money going into DAFs is essentially subtracted from other charitable giving." (Note the hedging in the use of words like "largely" and "essentially." Cantor states that the "awkward truth" is that "many [hedging again] DAF accounts go years [id.] without making a single distribution." He goes beyond supporting a mandatory payout for donor-advised funds and advocates granting all money represented by a gift to a fund within five years.

Those contemplating establishment of a donor-advised fund should at least be aware of the elements of this ongoing debate.

There are two other pending controversies that the budding philanthropist should at least contemplate. One is the fact that a private foundation may make grants to a donor-advised fund in satisfaction of its mandatory payout requirement. This state of affairs has its critics, who are unhappy that there is no payout requirement imposed on the donor-advised fund. The foundation thus obtains a payout credit for these grants, even though the money may not be distributed from the fund for some time.

The third controversy pertains to the fact that grants from donor-advised funds are forms of public support to some publicly supported charities (as discussed in Chapter 5). The Department of the Treasury and the IRS are known to be sensitive to the notion that a donor-advised fund may be merely a "conduit" of funds paid in by a donor or grantor where the purpose of the transfer is to "cleanse" (I avoided use of the word *launder*) the funds by making all of the money public support, where a payment directly by a donor or grantor to the publicly supported charity would be public support only in part.

The Department of the Treasury and the IRS are crafting tax regulations to regulate the use of donor-advised funds. These and other issues will likely be addressed by these regulations.

The Giving USA Foundation, in early 2018, published a report on donor-advised funds, stating that they are "one of the fastest-growing giving vehicles." (The case can be made that these funds are *the* fastest-growing charitable giving vehicles.) This report concludes that donor-advised funds are "here to stay for the foreseeable future."

Advantages and Disadvantages

Again, like most situations, the use of donor-advised funds presents advantages and disadvantages.

Here are the advantages associated with donor-advised funds:

- *Advantage #1*: One of the biggest advantages of the donor-advised fund is the simplicity associated with it. Unlike a private foundation or a public charity, there is no need to establish a legal entity in the form of an organization. No corporation, trust, or the like is required. Thus, there is no formation and cultivation of a governing board, election of officers, supervision of employees, conduct of board and committee meetings, preparation and maintenance of meeting minutes, record-keeping, and the like.

- *Advantage #2*: The donor-advised fund can be started with much less money than is the case with respect to the private foundation or the public charity. A front-page article in the February 12, 1998 *Wall Street Journal* ran with this headline: "You Don't Have to Be a Rockefeller to Set Up Your Own Foundation." Guess what the article was about!

- *Advantage #3*: To continue with this theme of simplicity, there are no annual reporting requirements, either to the IRS or one or more states. The sponsoring organization assumes the responsibility for that.

- *Advantage #4*: The donor-advised fund provides the "look and feel" of a private foundation, giving the donor the appearance of an institutionalized philanthropist. The grant check comes from a charitable fund rather than an individual.

- *Advantage #5*: The private foundation rules do not apply, except for the excess business holdings rules, which are not likely to be involved in any event. There is, however, the possibility that, in the coming years, a payout requirement will be imposed on donor-advised funds.

- *Advantage #6*: Contributions to sponsoring organizations, for the establishment and maintenance of a donor-advised fund, are contributions to public charities, not private foundations, so the more preferential charitable contribution rules are available.

- *Advantage #7*: Donors are free to make additional contributions to their donor-advised funds.

- *Advantage #8*: As a corollary to the previous advantage, donors can use donor-advised funds to smooth out their annual giving. If a donor is having a good year financially, the donor can make substantial contributions to the fund. If a tight year is underway, the donor can reduce or eliminate giving to the fund.

- *Advantage #9*: Donors are free to establish more than one donor-advised fund with a sponsoring organization or can establish one or more funds with one or more other sponsoring organizations.

- *Advantage #10*: Other persons can make contributions to a donor's donor-advised fund.

- *Advantage #11*: Funds distributed from donor-advised funds are forms of public support, which can be quite helpful if the grantees need that type of support to maintain their public charity status.

Here are the disadvantages associated with donor-advised funds:

- *Disadvantage #1*: The donor to a donor-advised fund loses control and other dominion over the contributed funds or other property to the sponsoring organization. This factor is ameliorated to the degree the sponsoring organization adheres to the advice tendered by the donor or the donor advisor.
- *Disadvantage #2*: There is no opportunity with a donor-advised fund to afford the donor or anyone else with employment. The law in this regard is more strict than that with respect to private foundations, which is more strict than that with respect to public charities.
- *Disadvantage #3*: A donor-advised fund cannot (without incurring a penalty tax) make a grant to an individual.
- *Disadvantage #4*: If the sponsoring organization is a community foundation, the grantees of the donor-advised fund may be confined to those in the community served by the foundation.
- *Disadvantage #5*: Although this does not happen frequently, donors can anonymously fund the charities they wish to support through donor-advised funds, by (of course) giving the funds a general name (e.g., the Clio Support Fund).
- *Disadvantage # 6*: Complex laws can operate to ensnare sponsoring organizations and their fund managers in costly taxable distributions rules.
- *Disadvantage #7*: Sponsoring organizations are prohibited by the tax law from making political campaign expenditures. Thus, money is donor-advised funds can't be used for that purpose.

Chapter 5
Public Charities

The vast majority of charities in the United States are public charities. There are hundreds of thousands of them. By contrast, there are about 90,000 private foundations. Thus, obviously, for most charities, public charity status is the way to go.

What Are *Public Charities*?
The simple answer to this question is that a public charity is a tax-exempt charitable organization that is not a private foundation (the latter being the subject of Chapter 3). Every charity in the U.S. is presumed, by the federal tax law, to be a private foundation. Thus, every charitable entity must either rebut that presumption and thereby become public or exist as a private foundation.

Three principal types of charitable organizations are not private foundations and thus are public charities:

- The *institutions* of the charitable world
- The *publicly supported charities*
- *Supporting organizations*

To avoid being a private foundation, an organization must demonstrate public involvement, public financial support, or an operating relationship with one or more public (or certain other types of) organizations.

Institutions

The federal tax law identifies certain nonprofit institutions in the charitable sector that are exempted from the private foundation rules and (usually) taxes:

- Churches, including synagogues and mosques. To qualify under this category of institution, a religious organization must have a place of worship and a congregation that meets on a regular basis. It likely will have other functions, such as the conduct of weddings and baptisms and operation of schools, but it is required to have those three core attributes. Consequently, organizations that conduct their services online or by telephone cannot be churches for tax law purposes.
- Other religious organizations, such as conventions and associations of churches, missionary societies, monasteries, nunneries, and retreat facilities.
- Operating educational institutions. This includes schools, colleges, and universities. These entities must have a formal place of instruction, as well as a faculty, curriculum, and student body.
- Operating health care providers, principally hospitals.
- Medical research organizations. These organizations engage in forms of medical research in direct conjunction with the activities of tax-exempt hospitals.
- Agricultural research organizations. These entities, modeled after medical research organizations, operate in tandem with land-grant and similar exempt colleges and universities.
- Governmental units, whether federal, state, or local.

There can be overlaps and affiliations here. Some schools and hospitals are governmental entities. A university campus can include a hospital or similar medical center. A church can have a related school. Other types of entities that are generally regarded as institutions, such as museums and libraries, do not have specific classification as public charity institutions. We will see how they otherwise achieve public charity status or perhaps are structured as private operating foundations (see Chapter 3).

Publicly Supported Charities

One of the chief characteristics of a private foundation is that, as noted, it is funded from one source. By contrast, one way for a charitable organization to be classified as a public charity is to draw its financial support from many sources, namely, the public.

There are two basic types of publicly supported organizations. The law has not assigned either of them a name. We will do that here:

- Donative publicly supported charities, which have heavy reliance on gifts and grants
- Service-provider publicly supported charities, which tend to have considerable fee-for-service revenue

These classifications can be oversimplified and perhaps somewhat artificial. Many publicly supported charities receive blends of contributions, grants, and fee-for-service revenue, not to mention investment income. But these categories are separately identified in the tax law; I will dutifully follow suit.

Donative Charities

A donative publicly supported charity is a charity that normally receives a substantial part of its financial support from direct and/or indirect contributions from the public, or from one or more governmental units in the form of grants. Key words in the foregoing sentence are *normally*, *substantial*, *direct*, *indirect*, *public*, and *grant*.

Most donative charities must receive at least one-third of their financial support—termed the *support ratio*—from eligible public or governmental sources. The time span for measuring the organization's support is its most recent five years— the *support computation period*—which is what the word *normally* means in this context. As noted below, this approach can prove tricky, in that the last of the years of the support computation period is the year (often not yet ended) in which the computation is being made.

Public support is derived from individuals, trusts, corporations, and other legal entities, including private foundations. (*Private* foundations can provide *public* support.) The total amount of contributions from any one donor or grants from any one grantor during the support computation period usually is not public support to the extent that the amount exceeds 2 percent of the organization's total support received during that period. This 2 percent limitation generally does not apply, however, to support received from other donative organizations or governmental units.

Donors who have a defined relationship with one another, such as husband and wife and a business and its sole owner, must share a single 2 percent limitation. Multiple contributions from any one source are aggregated over the support computation period.

When it is identifying income in the computation of its support ratio, an organization cannot include amounts received from the exercise or performance of its tax-exempt functions. An organization will not, however, meet the *support test* if it receives almost all of its support from its related activities and only an insignificant amount from governmental units and/or the public.

An organization's lawyer or accountant should be consulted on whether the support-ratio test requirements have been met. A formula fraction called a *support fraction* will be applied by the professional, using the organization's specific revenues in each category.

Here is an illustration as to how these rules work. A charitable organization received, during its most recent five years, the total sum in the form of gifts and grants of $400,000. Thus, to qualify as this type of public charity, its public support must be at least $134,000 (one-third of $400,000). To see whether that goal was met, the charity applies the 2 percent rule. Two percent of $400,000 is $8,000. Thus, as a general rule, support from a donor or grantor will be public support for this charity to the extent that that the amount is no more than $8,000. That is, a donor who gave $5,000 provided $5,000 in public support; a donor who gave $10,000 provided $8,000 in public support. Funds from other donative charities or government entities (if grants) are not limited by the 2 percent rule; that is, all the funds of this nature are forms of public support. Each donor's gift must be evaluated in this fashion to determine whether the $134,000 minimum goal was reached. One outcome might be 15 donors who gave $8,000 each (a total of $120,000) and a $20,000 government grant, resulting in $140,000 of public support—and satisfaction of the test.

An organization that meets a public support test for its current tax year is treated as a publicly supported entity for that year and the immediately succeeding tax year. For example, a calendar-year organization that meets a public support test for 2018, based on the five-year computation period 2014–2018, is a public charity for 2018 and 2019. If this organization cannot meet a public support test for 2018, based on the computation period consisting of 2014–2018, it nonetheless will be a public charity for 2018 because it met a public support test for 2017, based on the computation period of 2013–2017. If, however, the organization cannot meet a public support test for 2019, based on the 2015–2019 computation period, the organization will become a private foundation as of January 1, 2020. Because an organization that cannot meet a public support test for its current tax year is at risk of classification as a private foundation as of the first day of its subsequent tax year, the IRS has observed that organizations "may wish to carefully monitor their public support calculations."

Issues that may emerge in computing public support under these rules include whether the totality of support from an entity may be treated as public support, a payment is a grant (included in the support ratio) or made pursuant to a contract (excluded from the ratio), a payment can be excluded from the ratio because it qualifies as an unusual (unexpected) grant or gift, and whether the charity is eligible to use the facts-and-circumstances test (see below).

Service-Provider Charities

A service-provider charitable organization normally receives more than one-third of its support from gifts and grants, membership fees, and/or gross receipts from the performance of exempt functions. Amounts that are eligible are derived from *permitted sources*: governmental agencies, the three basic types of institutions (churches, educational institutions, and health care/medical research entities), donative charities, and persons who are not disqualified persons.

Also, to qualify as a service-provider charitable organization, no more than one-third of the organization's support can come from investment income.

Like the donative organizations rules, the service-provider organizations rules measure support over the most recent five years and utilize a one-third support fraction.

There are, however, some major differences between these two sets of law. Exempt function revenue can count as public support for the service-provider organization, but only to the extent that the revenue from any one source does not exceed the greater of $5,000 or 1 percent of the organization's support for the year involved.

The rules limit gifts and grants to service-provider charitable organizations. Public support cannot come from *disqualified persons*: an organization's directors and officers, members of their families, any controlled person, or a substantial contributor (whether an individual, trust, estate, corporation, or other entity). A *substantial contributor* is a person who contributes or bequeaths an aggregate amount of more than $5,000, where that amount is more than 2 percent of the total contributions in addition to bequests received by the organization.

Here is an example (as similar to the previous one as possible) illustrating how these rules work. A charitable organization received, during its most recent five years, the total sum, in the form of gifts and grants, of $400,000. Thus, to qualify as this type of public charity, its public support must be at least $134,000 (one-third of $400,000). To determine whether that goal was met, the charity subtracts gifts made by disqualified persons from its total gifts. Each donor's gift must be evaluated in this fashion to determine whether the $134,000 minimum goal was reached. One outcome might be 15 donors, none of whom are disqualified persons, who gave $8,000 each (a total of $120,000) and a $20,000 government grant, resulting in $140,000 of public support—and satisfaction of the test. Or, the $20,000 may have been in the form of qualifying exempt function revenue.

Issues that can arise in computing public support in this context are determining whether or not a person is a disqualified person, whether a payment is a gift or contract amount, and whether a payment is an unusual grant. The facts-and-circumstances test is not applicable in this setting.

Supporting Organizations

The third category of charitable organization that is not a private foundation is the *supporting organization*, an entity that is related, structurally or operationally, to one or more institutions, publicly supported organizations, or certain noncharitable organizations (namely, social welfare or labor organizations or business leagues). These beneficiary organizations are collectively referred to, not very imaginatively, as supported organizations. A supporting organization must be organized, and at all times operated exclusively for the benefit of, to perform the functions of, or to carry out the purposes of one or more supported organizations.

Supporting organizations in general can be versatile. They are used as fundraising vehicles, holders of endowments, managers of investment or other property, and entities that operate discrete programs. As noted below, however, law changes have not been for the better, with utilization of supporting organizations curbed in several ways.

Types of Supporting Organizations

The relationship between a supporting organization and a supported organization must be one of four types; the nature of the required interaction between the entities is likely to vary with each type of supporting organization:

- *Type I.* This type of supporting organization is operated, supervised, or controlled by one or more supported organizations, typically by giving the supported organization(s) the power to regularly appoint or elect a majority of the directors of the supporting organization. There is substantial direction of policies, programs, and activities of the supporting organization by the supported organization(s). This arrangement is akin to that of parent and subsidiary.
- *Type II.* This type of supporting organization is supervised or controlled in connection with one or more supported organizations. There is com-

mon control or management by the individuals heading both the supporting organization and the supported organization(s). This arrangement is
similar to the "brother-sister" relationship.

- *Type III, functionally integrated.* This type of supporting organization is operated in connection with one or more supported organizations. Its programs
are functionally integrated with those of the supported organization(s).

- *Type III, nonfunctionally integrated.* This type of supporting organization is
operated in connection with one or more supported organizations. It must
satisfy an attentiveness requirement and is subject to a mandatory payout
requirement.

A supporting organization may not be controlled directly or indirectly by one or
more disqualified persons.

In 2006, Congress imposed more law, much of it rather intricate, on and in
connection with supporting organizations. Some of this law involved application of
certain of the private foundation rules to supporting organizations (see below).
Other law brought specific application of the intermediate sanctions rules. The most
stringent provisions of the additional law are directed at Type III supporting organizations, particularly those that are not functionally integrated with one or more
supported organizations.

A grant-making private foundation (as contrasted with a private operating
foundation) may not treat as a qualifying distribution (see discussion following) an
amount paid to a Type III supporting organization that is not a functionally integrated Type III supporting organization or to any other type of supporting organization if a disqualified person with respect to the foundation directly or indirectly
controls the supporting organization or a supported organization of the supporting
organization. An amount that does not count as a qualifying distribution under this
rule is regarded as a taxable expenditure (see discussion following).

An organization is not considered to be operated, supervised, or controlled by
a qualified supported organization (the general criterion for a Type I organization)
or operated in connection with a supported organization (the general criterion for
Type IIIs) if the organization accepts a contribution from a person (other than a
qualified supported organization) who, directly or indirectly, controls, either alone
or with family members and/or certain controlled entities, the governing board of
a supported organization. A supporting organization is considered not to be operated
in connection with a supported organization unless the supporting organization is

operated only in connection with one or more supported organizations that are organized in the United States.

The private foundation excess business holdings rules (see discussion following) are applicable to Type III supporting organizations, other than functionally integrated Type III supporting organizations. The IRS has the authority, however, to exempt excess holdings from this tax regime where the holdings are consistent with the supporting organization's exempt function.

These excess business holdings rules also apply to a Type II supporting organization if the organization accepts a contribution from a person (other than a public charity that is not a supporting organization) who controls, either alone or with family members and/or certain controlled entities, the governing body of a supported organization of the supporting organization. Again, the IRS has the authority to refrain from imposing the excess business holdings rules on a supporting organization if the organization establishes that the holdings are consistent with the organization's tax-exempt status.

A Type III supporting organization must provide each organization that it supports information regarding the supporting organization in order to ensure the responsiveness by the supporting organization to the needs or demands of the supported organization(s). A Type III supporting organization may not support a foreign organization.

An entity is a Type III supporting organization if, in addition to the foregoing two rules, it satisfies a notification requirement, a responsiveness test, and an integral part test. There are, as the law would have it, two integral part tests, one for Type III functionally integrated supporting organizations and one for Type III non-functionally integrated organizations. These two tests are satisfied by maintaining significant involvement in the operations of the supported organization(s) and providing support on which the supported organization(s) are dependent. The notification requirement entails an annual provision of certain documents by the supporting organization to its supported organization(s).

The responsiveness test is met by the presence of interlocking board memberships and/or officer relationships with the organizations and a showing that the directors and officers of the supported organization have a significant voice in the supporting organization's investment policies, the timing of grants, the manner of making grants, and the selection of grant recipients.

A functionally integrated Type III supporting organization is a Type III supporting organization that is not required to grant funds to one or more supported organizations. The integral part test for functionally integrated Type III supporting organizations is met if the entity engages in activities substantially all of which directly further the exempt purposes of one or more supported organizations, it is the parent of each of its supported organizations, or it supports a governmental supported organization. As to the first of the ways to meet this integral part test, the supporting organization must perform the functions of or carry out the purposes of supported organizations and engage in activities that, but for its involvement, would be engaged in by the supported organizations. Activities that directly further the exempt purposes of supported organizations must be those that are conducted by the supporting organization. Generally, however, fundraising, grant-making, and investing and managing non-exempt-use assets are not activities that directly further exempt purposes.

The integral part test for non-functionally integrated Type III supporting organizations generally is satisfied if the entity meets a distribution requirement and an attentiveness requirement. Generally, the mandatory payout is the greater of 85 percent of adjusted gross income or an amount equal to 3.5 percent of the value of non-exempt use assets. The attentiveness requirement requires distribution of at least one-third of the organization's distributable amount to one or more supported organizations that are attentive to the operations of the supporting organization and to which the supporting organization is responsive. There are different ways to demonstrate this attentiveness, such as by providing at least 10 percent of the supported organization's total support or a showing that support from the supporting organization is necessary to avoid interruption of the carrying on of an activity of the supported organization.

An excise tax is imposed on disqualified persons if they engage in one or more excess benefit transactions with public charities and/or social welfare organizations. (This rule is part of the intermediate sanctions regime, which is somewhat akin to the private foundation self-dealing rules (see Chapter 3).) A grant, loan, compensation, or other similar payment (such as an expense reimbursement) by any type of supporting organization to a substantial contributor or a person related to a substantial contributor, as well as a loan provided by a supporting organization to certain disqualified persons with respect to the supporting organization, is automatically an excess benefit transaction. Thus, the entire amount paid to the substantial contributor, disqualified persons, and related parties is an excess benefit.

A supporting organization must annually demonstrate that one or more of its disqualified persons (other than its managers and supported organization(s)) do not, directly or indirectly, control it. This is done by means of a certification on its annual information return.

Supporting organizations are among the most useful and creative planning options in the realm of tax-exempt organizations. They can be used, for example, as a home for an endowment fund, a form of fundraising foundation, an entity in which programs may be conducted, a vehicle for holding title to property, an entity to receive large contributions so as to not disturb the parent's publicly supported charity status, or the basis by which a private foundation converts to a public charity. (The law changes made in 2006, however, have considerably eroded the versatility of the supporting organization.)

Planning Considerations

A charitable organization that is trying to avoid classification as a private foundation may need to do some solid financial planning, especially if the goal is to be a publicly supported organization. For organizations that desire to be regarded as publicly supported (essentially the donative and service-provider charities), however, the matter can be somewhat more complicated than for institutions or organizations that intend to be classified as supporting organizations.

An organization that can expect to receive nearly all of its support in the form of many relatively small gifts will have no trouble in achieving either donative or service-provider status. An organization that is essentially dues based will be a service provider, although not a donative entity. An organization that anticipates receiving most of its financial support as exempt function revenue must look to the category of service provider (rather than donative) organization, for relief from the private foundation rules. The reverse is probably true for an organization that is relying largely on government grants (as opposed to contracts) for support; it will look to the donative organization category.

Many organizations, during their formative years, rely on just a few sources of financial support (for example, one or more private foundations or makers of large gifts). For these entities, compliance with either the donative organization rules or the service-provider organization rules can be difficult (if not impossible). Under the service-provider organization rules, because their sources of support are likely to be substantial contributors, none of their support is eligible for treatment as public support. The outcome will be more favorable where the donative organization rules are applied: At least the amount received from each of these sources up to the 2 percent threshold can count as public support.

Compliance with either the donative organization rules or the service-provider organization rules at any time is all that is required. An organization is not locked in to one set of these rules or the other.

There is another dimension of this matter of public charity status that is sometimes overlooked. It pertains to those charities that receive (or want to receive) private foundation grants. As discussed further on, a private foundation can be taxed if it makes a taxable expenditure. One way to have this type of an expenditure is for a private foundation to make a grant to a charity that is not a public charity. If a private foundation makes a grant to a charity, thinking it is a donative organization or a service-provider organization and it is neither, there can be some serious adverse tax consequences (not to mention the termination of that private foundation's support for that grantee).

Additional Options

A charitable organization may not be able to satisfy the requirements of the general rules pertaining to institutions, publicly supported (donative or service-provider) organizations, or supporting organizations. There remain alternatives to private foundation status, or ways to alleviate some of the stringencies of the private foundation rules.

Facts-and-Circumstances Test

Some organizations generically are not private foundations; yet, they come within the broad reach of that term under the federal tax law. These organizations can include museums, libraries, and other entities that have substantial endowment funds. Some of these organizations may nonetheless be able to gain nonprivate-foundation status by means of the *facts-and-circumstances* test.

To meet this test, an organization must demonstrate that

- the total amount of public support it receives (calculated using the donative charity rules) is at least 10 percent of its total support;
- it has a continuous and bona fide program for the solicitation of funds from the public, governmental units, or other public charities; and
- it has other attributes of a public organization.

Among its other attributes, an organization might reference the composition of its governing board (showing how it is representative of the public), the extent to which its facilities or programs are publicly available, its membership dues rates, and how its activities are likely to appeal to persons having some broad common interest or purpose.

The higher the percentage of public support, the easier the burden of establishing the publicly supported nature of the organization through the other factors.

The main point to be emphasized, however, is that under this test the organization's public support need only be as little as 10 percent of its total support, rather than having to be at least one-third of the total support under the general rules.

Bifurcation

An organization that is—or might be classified by the IRS as—a private foundation may be able to avoid that consequence by bifurcating into two entities. Each of the two organizations may be able to qualify as a nonfoundation, where they could not do so if combined.

An organization may have within it a function that, if separately evaluated, would qualify as an institution, a donative publicly supported organization, or a service-provider publicly supported organization. This function could be spun off into a separate organization and qualified as a public entity. The original organization, with its remaining activities, could then become qualified as a supporting organization with respect to its offspring. In this way, one private organization becomes two public organizations.

For example, suppose an individual established a private foundation for educational purposes. Over time, the foundation begins providing direct instruction to students. The board of trustees would like the foundation to remain in existence. The trustees convert the direct-instruction part of the foundation into an operating educational institution – a school with a faculty, student body, and curricula. That organization gains classification as a public charity—one of the institutions. The remaining part of the foundation, with the original board of trustees, is converted into a supporting organization for the school. The foundation board remains in place; the organization itself is now a public charity.

Private Operating Foundation

In some instances, the private operating foundation is the way to go. Being a hybrid between a public charity, many of the advantages associated with both categories are available. These entities are discussed in Chapter 3.

Advocacy Efforts

Organizations that are tax exempt because they are charitable in nature (including educational, scientific, religious, and similar entities (see Chapter 2)) must, to preserve the exemption, adhere to a variety of requirements. One of these requirements states that "no substantial part of the activities" of the organization may constitute "carrying on propaganda, or otherwise attempting, to influence legislation." There is considerable and continuing uncertainty as to the meaning and scope of this rule, unimaginatively termed the *substantial part test*, not the least of which is the meaning of the word *substantial*.

Legislation applicable to most public charities entails a system of excise taxes on excess lobbying outlays. Under these rules, if a charitable organization loses its tax exemption because of attempts to influence legislation, a tax of 5 percent of the *lobbying expenditures* is imposed on the organization. (This tax *does not apply* to any organization that is under the expenditure test described below or that is ineligible to make that election.) A lobbying expenditure is any amount paid or incurred by a charitable organization in carrying on propaganda or otherwise attempting to influence legislation.

A separate 5 percent tax is applicable to each of the organization's managers (its officers, directors, and key employees) who agreed to the lobbying expenditures (knowing they were likely to result in revocation of its exemption), unless the agreement was not willful and was due to reasonable cause. The burden of proof for whether a manager knowingly participated in the lobbying expenditure is on the IRS. The imposition of an excise tax on an organization does not itself establish that any manager of the organization is subject to the excise tax.

In response to this intolerable situation concerning the vagueness of the word *substantial*, Congress enacted another test, the *expenditure test*, which utilizes a tax system as well, although none of the taxes fall on individuals involved. These rules are not a substitute for the general rules (embodied in the substantial part test) but serve as a "safe harbor" guideline, so that a charitable organization that is in compliance with the expenditure test is deemed to be in conformance with the general rules.

These rules are termed *elective* because charitable organizations must elect to come under these standards. Organizations that choose not to make the election remain governed by the substantial part test, with its uncertainties. Churches, conventions or associations of churches, integrated auxiliaries of churches, certain supporting organizations, and private foundations (with their own rules on the point) may not elect to come under the expenditure test.

The expenditure test rules provide a definition of terms such as *legislation, influencing legislation, direct lobbying*, and *grassroots lobbying*. These terms are essentially the same as those used in connection with the substantial part test. (The test also provides some exemptions from its purview.) In an attempt to define when the legislative process begins (and, therefore, when a lobbying process begins), however, the expenditure test offers a definition of legislative *action:* the "introduction, amendment, enactment, defeat, or repeal of Acts, bills, resolutions, or similar items."

The expenditure test measures permissible and impermissible legislative activities of charitable organizations in terms of sets of declining percentages of total exempt purpose expenditures. (These do not include fundraising expenses.) The basic permitted annual level of expenditures for legislative efforts (termed the *lobbying nontaxable amount*) is 20 percent of the first $500,000 of an organization's expenditures for an exempt purpose (including legislative activities), plus 15 percent of the next $500,000, 10 percent of the next $500, 000, and 5 percent of any remaining expenditures. The total amount spent for legislative activities in any one year by an electing charitable organization may not exceed $1 million. A separate limitation— amounting to one-fourth of the foregoing amounts—is imposed on grassroots lobbying expenditures.

Here is where some other taxes come in. A charitable organization that has elected these limitations and exceeds either the general lobbying ceiling amount or the grassroots lobbying ceiling amount becomes subject to an excise tax of 25 percent of the excess lobbying expenditures. The tax falls on the greater of the two excesses. If an electing organization's lobbying expenditures normally (an average over a four-year period) exceed 150 percent of either limitation, it will lose its tax-exempt status as a charitable organization.

As is the case with private foundations, exceptions from these rules are available for public charities. If the charity is under the substantial part test, there is no taxation and no endangerment of tax exemption if the organization only engages in nonpartisan analysis, study, or research (that is, activities that are educational) or is testifying about a legislative proposal in response to an invitation from a legislative committee. More true exceptions are available in connection with the expenditure test: (1) making available nonpartisan analysis, study, or research; (2) providing technical advice or assistance; (3) the self-defense exception (see Chapter 3); (4) communications between the organization and its members with respect to legislation of direct interest; and (5) routine communications with government officials or employees.

Fundraising Regulation

Government regulation of fundraising traditionally has been at the state level. Nearly every state has a form of a *charitable solicitation act*—a statute regulating fundraising for charitable purposes. Because of these laws, charities constantly face differing registration and reporting forms, accounting methods, due dates, bond requirements, enforcement attitudes, and other substantial twists in the states' regulatory regime. Many counties, cities, and towns compound the process with similar ordinances.

Essentially, then, a charitable organization engaged in fundraising must obtain permission in advance from each state involved before the charity can begin its solicitations. This permission is usually termed a *permit* or *license*, acquired as the result of filing a *registration*. The staff time and expense required to obtain and maintain these registrations throughout the states can be enormous. These laws often also mandate registration, reporting, and the like by professional fundraisers and professional solicitors.

Federal regulation of charitable fundraising largely takes place within the tax system. The charitable deduction rules (Chapter 7) operate as a form of fundraising regulation. More so, however, are the procedural (or administrative) rules that accompany the substantive charitable deduction rules. These are the laws governing recordkeeping, gift substantiation, the obtaining of appraisals, and reporting rules (also summarized in Chapter 7).

In addition to state and federal regulation, fundraising for charitable ends can cause a public charity to be scrutinized by one or more nonprofit organizations that are self-styled watchdog agencies. These organizations take it as their responsibility to evaluate and report on the fundraising and other functions of these charities. This is done in the name of consumer protection—shielding the unsuspecting public from the machinations of abusive, unethical, and unscrupulous, if not downright fraudulent, fundraising organizations. Some of these watchdogs go further and rate fundraising charities. Their criteria for doing so varies from organization to organization, and they are sometimes unreasonable and unfair. Prospective donors, the media, and governments tend to unquestioningly rely on these reports and ratings. Public charities with fundraising programs prudently regard these groups warily; a bad rating can destroy a fundraising effort—and maybe the charity itself.

Intermediate Sanctions Rules

Intermediate sanctions are termed *intermediate* because they are imposed on directors, officers, key employees, or other types of disqualified persons who engage in inappropriate private transactions (rather than the exempt organization).

The heart of this body of tax law is the *excess benefit transaction*. A transaction is considered an excess benefit transaction if an economic benefit is provided by an applicable tax-exempt organization directly or indirectly to, or for the use of, a disqualified person, if the value of the economic benefit provided exceeds the value of the consideration received by the exempt organization for providing the benefit. Those that have avoided law school may be unfamiliar with this notion of *consideration*. The concept is at the heart of the law of contracts, which requires that an agreement be based on adequate consideration received by the parties to be enforceable. Consideration is what each party to the agreement derives from the deal; it is supposed to be roughly equal.

The principal focus of intermediate sanctions is on instances of unreasonable compensation—where a person's level of compensation is deemed to be in excess of the value of the economic benefit derived by the organization from the person's services. Like the private inurement doctrine, however, these sanctions also potentially extend to lending and rental arrangements, property sales, and the like.

The concept of the excess benefit transaction includes any transaction in which the amount of any economic benefit provided to, or for the use of, a disqualified person is determined in whole or in part by the revenues of one or more activities of the organization, where the transaction is reflected in tax regulations and results in private inurement.

A *disqualified person* generally is any person who was, at any time during the five-year period ending on the date of the transaction, in a position to exercise substantial influence over the affairs of the organization. The term *disqualified person* also includes members of the family of someone who is a disqualified person under the general rule and organizations (corporations, partnerships, trusts) in which these persons own more than 35 percent of the stock or other interest.

A disqualified person who benefited from an excess benefit transaction is subject to an initial tax equal to 25 percent of the amount of the excess benefit. Moreover, this person will be required to return the excess benefit amount to the tax-exempt organization. An *organization manager* (usually a director or officer) who participated in an excess benefit transaction, knowing that it was such a transaction, is subject to an initial tax of 10 percent of the excess benefit. An additional tax may be imposed on a disqualified person where the initial tax was imposed and the appropriate correction of the excess benefit transaction did not occur. In this situation, the disqualified person is subject to a tax equal to 200 percent of the excess benefit involved.

A fascinating (and huge) exception to the intermediate sanctions rules is the *initial contract* exception. These rules do not apply to a fixed payment made by an applicable tax-exempt organization to a disqualified person pursuant to the first contract between the parties. A *fixed payment* is an amount of money or other property specified in the contract involved, or determined by a fixed formula specified in the contract, which is to be paid or transferred in exchange for the provision of specified services or property. An *initial contract* is a binding written contract between an applicable tax-exempt organization and a person who was not a disqualified person immediately prior to entering into the contract. (This exception is informally referred to as the *first bite* exception, the parallel drawn with the law of dogs.)

If a transaction creating a benefit was approved by an independent board, or an independent committee of the board, a presumption arises that the terms of the transaction are reasonable, where the decision was based on appropriate data and was timely documented. The burden of proof would then shift to the IRS, which would then have to overcome (rebut) the presumption to prevail. This presumption may cause a restructuring of the boards of directors or trustees of many charitable organizations.

Advantages and Disadvantages

Like the other choices, public charity status has its advantages and disadvantages. There are many advantages to public charity status; it is tough to rank them.

Here are the advantages to public charity status:

- *Advantage #1.* Let's focus on this matter of *control*, since it is such a dominant one. Yes, as a matter of law, a donor can create and control a public charity. But not all of them (see below). In other instances, although this type of control may be lawful, it is not likely to materialize or, if it does, be maintained.
- *Advantage #2:* The charitable giving rules are tilted in favor of public charities (see Chapter 7). Particularly where gifts of property other than publicly traded securities are concerned, public charity status is clearly a preferable position to be in compared to private foundation status or use of a donor-advised fund.
- *Advantage #3:* A donor can sometimes have it both ways by establishing and utilizing a supporting organization. Gifts to a supporting organization are eligible for the more generous charitable deduction rules, inasmuch as a supporting organization is a type of public charity. A donor is likely to

be a disqualified person with respect to the supporting organization, however, and thus be barred by law from controlling the organization. This lack-of-control factor can be offset, however, by having other board members (unrelated parties) be individuals the donor can trust and/or where the donor has a good relationship (but not a control relationship) with the supported organization or organizations.

- *Advantage #4*: Public charities, for the most part, do not have to cope with the private foundation rules. Somewhat offsetting this advantage is the fact that disqualified persons with respect to public charities are subject to the intermediate sanctions rules (see above).
- *Advantage #5*: Public charities have much more flexibility in engaging in and funding efforts to influence legislation than private foundations and donor-advised funds (see above).
- *Advantage #6*: Most types of public charities are able to establish and utilize supporting organizations.
- *Advantage #7*: Public charities may establish and utilize for-profit subsidiaries, usually to house unrelated business that would endanger their tax-exempt status if undertaken directly by them. Private foundations are blocked from using for-profit subsidiaries engaging in active business activities by reason of the excess business holdings rules.
- *Advantage #8*: Nearly all types of public charities are eligible to receive grants from private foundations. It is uncommon for a private foundation to make a grant to another private foundation.

Here are the disadvantages to public charity status:

- *Disadvantage #1*: Once the public charity is formed, the parties are usually locked in as to what the organization can do. For example, if the entity is a school or hospital, it is not likely to morph into some other type of organization. It can change form but that is not likely to happen.
- *Disadvantage #2*: Realistically, an individual is not likely to set up a public charity such as a bona fide church, school, hospital, or medical research organization. It happens, of course, but it is a complicated undertaking, certainly more difficult than forming a private foundation.
- *Disadvantage #3*: Establishment of a public charity is likely to entail formation of a relatively large board of directors or trustees. This fact not only

reduces or eliminates the likelihood that a donor will control the charity but introduces all the other complexities associated with establishing and maintaining a governing board (e.g., meetings, minutes, travel, compensation, and/or other expenses).

- *Disadvantage #4*: If the public charity is to be a supporting organization, there can be headaches. This is particularly true if the charity is to be a Type III supporting organization. Matters deteriorate further if the entity involved is a nonfunctionally integrated Type III supporting organization. The functions of this type of organization can be limited. Private foundations generate problems for themselves if they make grants to Type III supporting organizations—and sometimes avoid these problems by not making grants to any supporting organizations. Donor-advised funds are penalized if they make grants to disqualified supporting organizations.

- *Disadvantage #5*: Most public charities are required to engage in fundraising. Sometimes, fundraising is required as a matter of law, e.g., publicly supported charities. In other instances, fundraising is required as a matter of necessity, e.g., churches, schools, hospitals, and some supporting organizations. Fundraising, if done correctly, costs money—a lot of money. This requires investment in staff (often termed *development offices*), technology, lawyers (particularly where planned giving is concerned), and probably outside fundraising consultants. Charitable fundraising also brings the public charity within the ambit of state and federal fundraising regulation. Thinking extremely positively, however, fundraising can be seen as a plus; it can bring in stupendous sums of money to be applied to charitable programming.

- *Disadvantage #6*: Because of their complexity and size, public charities are usually the most expensive types of charities to form and maintain.

- *Disadvantage #7*: Public charities, particularly those engaging in fundraising, can attract the attention (and sometimes the wrath) of the watchdog agencies.

- *Disadvantage #8*: Public charities are not supposed to engage in political campaign activities. As noted, however, this prohibition also applies to private foundations and donor-advised funds.

Chapter 6

Unrelated Business Rules

For nearly 70 years, the federal tax law has divided the activities of tax-exempt organizations into two categories: (1) those that are related to the performance of exempt functions and (2) those that are not. The revenue occasioned by the latter activities, *unrelated activities*, although it can be used to support charitable activities, is subject to income tax.

Public charities (see Chapter 5) and the unrelated business rules co-exist rather well. Private foundations (see Chapter 3), however, must tread carefully. While it is possible for foundations to have unrelated business income, the ownership of active business enterprises is perilous, because of the excess business holdings rules.

Reason for These Rules

The unrelated income rules, enacted in 1950, were significantly augmented by Congress in 1969. The original concept underlying these rules was that of an *outside* business owned and perhaps operated by a tax-exempt organization. In 1969, however, Congress significantly expanded the reach of these rules by authorizing the IRS to evaluate activities conducted by nonprofit organizations internally—*inside* activities. This body of law has expanded exponentially ever since.

The objective of the unrelated business income tax law is to prevent unfair competition between tax-exempt organizations and for-profit, commercial enterprises. As the House Committee on Ways and Means observed during enactment of these rules, the "problem at which the tax on unrelated business income is directed here is primarily that of unfair competition," in that exempt organizations can "use their profits tax-free to expand operations, while their competitors can expand only with the profits remaining after taxes." The Senate Committee on Finance reaffirmed this position nearly three decades later when it noted that the "major purpose" of the unrelated business rules "is to make certain that an exempt organization does not commercially exploit its exempt status for the purpose of unfairly competing with taxpaying organizations."

The rules are intended to place the unrelated business activities of an exempt organization on the same tax basis as those of a nonexempt business with which it competes. It is often said that the purpose of the unrelated business income tax is to "level the playing field" as between competing nonprofit and for-profit organizations. One wag suggested, however, that for-profit businesses do not even want nonprofit entities *on* the field.

Overview

To be tax-exempt, a nonprofit organization must be organized and operated primarily for exempt purposes. The federal tax law allows an exempt organization to engage in a certain amount of income-producing activity that is unrelated to exempt purposes. Where the organization derives net income from one or more unrelated business activities, known formally as *unrelated business taxable income*, it is subject to tax on that income. An organization's tax exemption will be denied or revoked if an inappropriate portion of its activities is not promoting one or more of its exempt purposes.

Business activities may preclude the initial qualification of an otherwise tax-exempt organization. If the organization is not being operated principally for exempt purposes, it will fail the *operational test*. If its articles of organization empower it to carry on substantial activities that are not in furtherance of its exempt purpose, it will not meet the *organizational test*.

A nonprofit organization may still satisfy the operational test, even when it operates a business as a substantial part of its activities, as long as the business promotes the organization's exempt purpose. If the organization's primary purpose is carrying on a business for profit, it may be denied exemption on the grounds that it is a *feeder organization*, even if all of its profits are payable to one or more tax-exempt organizations.

Occasionally, the IRS will assume a different stance toward the tax consequences of one or more unrelated businesses when it comes to qualification for tax exemption. That is, the IRS may conclude that a business is unrelated and subject to the unrelated business income tax. Yet, the IRS may also agree that the purpose of the unrelated business is such that the activity helps further the organization's exempt function (funds are being generated for exempt purposes), even if the business activity is more than one-half of total operations. In this setting, then, the exempt organization can be in the anomalous position of having a considerable amount of taxable business activity—while still being tax-exempt.

Essentially, for an activity of a tax-exempt organization to be taxed, three tests must be satisfied. The activity (1) must constitute a *trade or business*, (2) be *regularly carried on*, (3) not be *substantially related* to the tax-exempt purposes of the organization. Many exceptions to these rules, however, exempt from taxation certain forms of activity and certain types of income.

The unrelated income rules are in a peculiar state of affairs these days. The courts are simultaneously developing additional and sometimes different criteria for assessing the presence of unrelated business, and from judicial decisions a doctrine of *commerciality* has emerged (see Chapter 2). This results in both considerable confusion as to what the law in this area is and extensive judgmental leeway on the part of the courts and the IRS in applying it.

Affected Exempt Organizations

Nearly all types of tax-exempt organizations are subject to the unrelated income rules. They include religious organizations (including churches), educational organizations (including universities, colleges, and schools), health care organizations (including hospitals), scientific organizations, and other charitable organizations. Beyond the realm of charitable entities, the rules are applicable to social welfare organizations (including advocacy groups), labor organizations (including unions), trade and professional associations, fraternal organizations, employee benefit funds, and veterans' organizations.

Certain organizations are not generally subject to the unrelated income rules, simply because they are not allowed to engage in any active business endeavors. This is the case, for example, for private foundations and title-holding organizations. Instrumentalities of the United States, like nearly all governmental agencies, are exempt from the unrelated business rules. The unrelated income rules are, however, applicable to colleges and universities that are agencies or instrumentalities of a government, as well as to corporations owned by these colleges and universities.

Definition of *Business*

For the purpose of the federal unrelated business rules, the term *trade or business* includes any activity that is carried on for the production of income from the sale of goods or the performance of services. Most activities that would constitute a trade or business under basic tax law principles are considered a trade or business for purposes of the unrelated income rules.

This definition of the term *trade or business* embraces nearly every activity of a tax-exempt organization; only passive investment activities generally escape this classification. In this sense, every exempt organization should be viewed as a bundle of activities, each of which is a trade or business. (It must be emphasized that this definition has nothing to do with whether an activity is related or unrelated; there are related businesses and unrelated businesses.)

The IRS is empowered to examine each of an organization's activities in search of unrelated business. Each activity can be examined as though it existed wholly independently of the others; an unrelated activity cannot, as a matter of law, be hidden from scrutiny by tucking it in among a cluster of related activities. As Congress chose to state the principle, an "activity does not lose identity as a trade or business merely because it is carried on within a larger aggregate of similar activities or within a larger complex of other endeavors which may, or may not, be related to the exempt purposes of the organization." This is known, in the jargon of tax law professionals, as the *fragmentation rule*. For example, the fragmentation rule allows the IRS to treat the income from the sale of advertising space in an exempt organization's magazine as revenue derived from an unrelated business, even though otherwise the publication of the magazine is a related business.

The federal tax law also states that "where an activity carried on for profit constitutes an unrelated trade or business, no part of such trade or business shall be excluded from such classification merely because it does not result in profit." In other words, just because an activity results in a loss in a year, that is insufficient basis for failing to treat the activity as an unrelated one (including reporting it as such to the IRS). Conversely, because the fact that an activity generates a profit is not alone supposed to lead to the conclusion that the activity is unrelated (although there are many in the IRS and on court benches who are likely to leap to that conclusion).

There is a problem here, nonetheless. An activity that consistently (over several consecutive years) results in losses will not be regarded as a *business*. If that is the only unrelated activity, that characterization is good news, because then it cannot be an *unrelated business*. Some tax-exempt organizations, however, have more than one unrelated business. They can offset the losses generated by one business against the gains enjoyed by another business in calculating unrelated business taxable income. But, if the loss activity is not a business to begin with, its losses cannot be credited against unrelated gain.

Just as *profits* are not built into the formal definition of the term *trade or business*, so too is the element of *unfair competition* missing from that definition. Yet, unfair competition is the driving force behind the unrelated income rules, and the IRS and the courts sometimes use the factor of competition in assessing whether an activity is related or unrelated to exempt functions.

Another absent term in the tax law definition of *trade or business* is *commerciality*. Nothing in the statutory law generally authorizes the IRS and judges to conclude that an activity is unrelated solely because it is conducted in a commercial manner, which basically means it is conducted the way a comparable activity is carried on by for-profit businesses. But the IRS does it anyway.

Concept of *Regularly Carried On*

To be considered an unrelated business, an activity must be *regularly carried on* by a tax-exempt organization.

Income from an activity is considered taxable only when (assuming the other criteria are satisfied) the activity is regularly carried on, as distinguished from sporadic or infrequent transactions. The factors that determine whether an activity is regularly carried on are the frequency and continuity of the activities, and the manner in which the activities are pursued. (In this context, the statutory law comes the closest to using a doctrine of *commerciality*.)

These factors must be evaluated in light of the purpose of the unrelated business income tax, which is to place tax-exempt organizations' business activities on the same tax basis as those of their nonexempt business competitors. Specific business activities of an exempt organization will generally be deemed to be regularly carried on if they are frequent and continuous and are pursued in a manner that is generally similar to comparable commercial activities of nonexempt organizations.

Where an organization duplicates income-producing activities performed by commercial organizations year-round, but performs those activities for a period of only a few weeks, they do not constitute the regular carrying on of a trade or business. Similarly, occasional or annual income-producing activities, such as fundraising events, do not amount to a business that is regularly carried on. The conduct of year-round business activities, such as the operation of a parking lot for one day each week, however, constitutes the regular carrying on of a business. Where commercial entities normally undertake income-producing activities on a seasonal basis, the conduct of the activities by an exempt organization during a significant portion of the season is deemed the regular conduct of that activity. For this purpose, a *season* may be a portion of the year (such as the summer) or a holiday period.

There are two problem areas to watch out for. Generally, the law, in ascertaining regularity, looks only at the time consumed in the actual conduct of the activity. The IRS, however, is of the view (not unreasonably) that time expended *preparing* for the event (*preparatory time*) should also be taken into account. This can convert what appears to be an exempted activity into a taxable business.

Outsourcing is a popular management tool these days. Tax-exempt organizations often try to outsource unrelated activities (and try to bring these profits in as nontaxable income, usually as royalties). This arrangement often entails a contract that sometimes casts the party with whom the exempt organization is contracting as the organization's *agent*. This is a bad idea. Under the law of *principal* and *agent*, the activities of the agent are attributed to the principal. Here, the exempt organization is the principal. To attribute the agent's activities to the exempt organization destroys any tax planning reasons for the relationship.

Unrelated Trade or Business

The term *unrelated trade or business* is defined to mean "any trade or business the conduct of which [by a tax-exempt organization] is not substantially related (aside from the need of such organization for income or funds or the use it makes of the profits derived) to the exercise or performance by such organization of its charitable, educational, or other purpose or function constituting the basis for its exemption." The parenthetical clause means that an activity is not related simply because the organization uses the net revenue from the activity for exempt purposes.

The revenue from a regularly conducted trade or business is subject to tax, unless the business activity is substantially related to the accomplishment of the organization's exempt purpose. The key to taxation or nontaxation in this area is the meaning of the words *substantially related*. Yet the law tells us merely that to be substantially related, the activity must have a *substantial causal relationship* to the accomplishment of an exempt purpose.

The fact that an asset is essential to the conduct of an organization's exempt activities does not shield from taxation the unrelated income produced by that asset. The income-producing activities must still meet the causal relationship test if the income is not to be subject to tax. This issue arises when a tax-exempt organization owns a facility or other assets that are put to a dual use. For example, the operation of an auditorium as a motion picture theater for public entertainment in the evenings is treated as an unrelated activity even though the theater is used exclusively for exempt purposes during the daytime hours. The fragmentation rule allows this type of use of a single asset to be split into two businesses.

Activities should not be conducted on a scale larger than is reasonably necessary for the performance of exempt functions. Activities in excess of the needs of exempt functions constitute unrelated businesses.

A host of court cases and IRS rulings provide illustrations of related and unrelated activities. Colleges and universities operate dormitories and bookstores as related activities but can be taxed on travel tours and sports camps. Hospitals may operate gift shops, snack bars, and parking lots as related activities but may be taxable on sales of pharmaceuticals to the public and on performance of routine laboratory tests for physicians. Museums may, without taxation, sell items reflective of their collections but are supposed to be taxable on the sale of souvenirs and furniture. Trade associations may find themselves taxable on sales of items and particular services to members, whereas dues and subscription revenue are nontaxable. Fundraising events may be characterized as unrelated activities, particularly when compensation is paid or when the activity is regularly carried on.

Unrelated Business Taxable Income

As noted earlier, to be subject to the unrelated income rules, an activity must satisfy (or, depending on one's point of view, fail) three tests. These tests are built into the definition of the term *unrelated business taxable income*: the "gross income derived by any [exempt] organization from any unrelated trade or business …regularly carried on by it, less the deductions allowed…[under federal tax law in general] which are directly connected with the carrying on of such trade or business."

The federal tax law as to computation of unrelated business taxable income was altered for tax years beginning after 2017. Tax-exempt organizations have been able to offset net income from an unrelated business with a loss from another unrelated business, assuming the loss position did not prevent the activity from failing to qualify as a business in the first instance. This practice came to a halt, however, when Congress enacted what I call the *bucketing* rule. (The idea is that each business activity, with its revenue and expenses, is in a separate bucket.)

Now, in the case of a tax-exempt organization with two or more unrelated businesses, unrelated business taxable income must be computed separately with respect to each business. The unrelated business taxable income for a year, for an exempt organization in this situation, is the sum of the amounts (not less than zero) computed for each unrelated business. A net operating loss deduction is allowed only with respect to a business from which the loss arose. Thus, a deduction from one unrelated business for a tax year may not be used to offset income from a different unrelated business for the same tax year.

Both this gross income and allowable deductions are computed in conformance with the *modifications* (see discussion following).

Some tax-exempt organizations are members of partnerships. If a trade or business regularly carried on by the partnership is an unrelated trade or business, the organization has special reporting requirements. In computing its unrelated business taxable income, it must (subject to the modifications) include its share (whether or not distributed) of the partnership's gross income from the unrelated business and its share of the partnership deductions directly connected with the gross income. (This is an application of what the tax law terms the *look-through rule*.) An exempt organization's share (whether or not distributed) of the gross income of a *publicly traded partnership* must be treated as gross income derived from an unrelated business, and its share of the partnership deductions is allowed in computing unrelated business taxable income.

A tax-exempt organization may own *debt-financed property*, and the use of the property may be unrelated to the organization's exempt function. When the organization computes its unrelated business taxable income, any income from the property has to be included as gross income derived from an unrelated business. The income is subject to tax in the same proportion that the property is financed by debt. The debt involved must be what the tax law terms *acquisition indebtedness*. The most common example is a mortgage.

Not every debt, however, that is associated with a property is an acquisition indebtedness. A payment obligation may be incurred by a tax-exempt organization solely for convenience in administering an exempt function and/or as part of ordinary and routine activities undertaken in the administration of investment properties. (There is no exemption from the debt-financed property rules for short-term borrowings as such.) Indeed, an amount involved may not be a *debt* in the first instance, that term meaning a fixed or determinable sum of money.

Exceptions for Activities

Despite the foregoing general rules, certain businesses conducted by tax-exempt organizations are exempted from taxation. A frequent exemption from taxation is a business "in which substantially all the work is performed for the organization without compensation." If an exempt organization conducts an unrelated business using services substantially provided by volunteers, the net revenue from that business is not taxable. This exemption protects from taxation many ongoing charitable fundraising activities. Caution must be exercised, however, because *compensation* is not confined to a salary, wage, or fee; the slightest amount of remuneration (such as tips) can nullify an individual's status as a *volunteer*.

Also exempted is a trade or business carried on by the organization "primarily for the convenience of its members, students, patients, officers, or employees." This exception is available, however, only to organizations that are charitable, educational, and the like, or are governmental colleges and universities.

A further exemption is given to a trade or business "which is the selling of merchandise, substantially all of which has been received by the organization as gifts or contributions." This exemption shelters the work of exempt thrift stores from taxation. Its use, though, is not confined to thrift shops. For example, it can protect auction revenue from taxation, even if auctions are regularly carried on. Similarly, the exception prevents charities that receive donated vehicles and then sell them from being considered in the unrelated business of dealing in automobiles, boats, and the like.

Exceptions for Income

Certain types of passive income and income derived from research are exempt from the unrelated business income tax.

Because the unrelated income tax applies to active businesses conducted by tax-exempt organizations, most types of passive income are exempt from taxation. This exemption generally covers dividends, interest, securities, loan payments, annuities, royalties, rent, capital gains, and gains on the lapse or termination of options written by exempt organizations.

There are, however, important exceptions to this exemption for passive income:

- Income in the form of rent, royalties, and the like from an active business undertaking is likely to be taxable, that is, merely labeling an income flow as rent, royalties, and so forth does not make it tax free.
- The unrelated debt-financed income rules override the general exemption for passive income.
- Interest, annuities, royalties, and rents from a controlled corporation may be taxable.

The following exemptions pertain to the conduct of research:

- Income derived from research for the United States or any of its agencies or instrumentalities, or for any state or political subdivision of a state.
- Income derived from research performed for any person at a college, university, or hospital.
- Income derived from research performed for any person at an organization operated primarily for purposes of carrying on fundamental research, the results of which are freely available to the public.

For the most part, the tax law is clear regarding what constitutes *dividends, interest,* an *annuity, rent,* and *capital gain.* There is, however, considerable controversy (reflected in many recent court opinions) concerning what constitutes a *royalty.* The term, not defined by statute or regulation, is being defined by the courts.

Generally, a *royalty* is a payment for the use of one or more valuable intangible property rights. In the tax-exempt organizations setting, this is likely to mean payment for the use of an organization's name and logo. The core issue usually is the extent to which the exempt organization receiving the (ostensible) royalty can provide services in an attempt to increase the amount of royalty income paid to it. This issue was the subject of extensive litigation spanning many years, principally involving revenue from the rental of mailing lists and revenue derived from affinity card programs. The resulting rule is that these services are permissible as long as they are insubstantial. Beyond that, the IRS may argue that the exempt organization is in a *joint venture*, which is an active business undertaking that defeats the exclusion.

Use of Subsidiaries

Some tax-exempt organizations elect to spin off their unrelated activities to related taxable subsidiaries. The tax on the net income of the unrelated activity is then not borne directly by the exempt organization. The managers of the tax-exempt organization may be averse to reporting any unrelated income, or the unrelated activity may be too large in relation to related activity.

If funds are transferred from a taxable subsidiary to an exempt parent, that income will generally be taxable as unrelated income to the parent if it is interest, rents, royalties, or annuities, where the parent has, directly or indirectly, more than 50 percent control of the subsidiary. If, however, the subsidiary pays dividends to the tax-exempt parent, the dividends are not taxable to the parent because they are not deductible by the subsidiary.

Calculating the Tax

For incorporated tax-exempt organizations, the net revenue from unrelated activities is subject to the regular federal corporate income tax. The federal tax on individuals applies to the unrelated activities of organizations that are not corporations (e.g., trusts). In determining net revenue, an exempt organization may deduct those expenses that are directly related to the conduct of unrelated business.

A specific deduction of $1,000 is available. This means that the first $1,000 of unrelated income is spared taxation. This deduction is taken into account only after the bucketing rule (see above) is applied.

Reporting Rules

A tax-exempt organization with unrelated business taxable income must file, in addition to an annual information return, a tax return (Form 990-T). On this return, the source or sources of unrelated income, and accompanying expenses, are reported, and any tax due is computed. As noted, the first $1,000 of annual net unrelated income is exempt from taxation. The organization's primary unrelated business activity must be described.

This tax return contains various schedules. One of these schedules concerns rental income. There, the rental property or properties must be described. Income derived from the rental of personal property must be reported if the percentage of rent for personal property is more than 10 percent but not more than 50 percent. Income derived from the rental of real and personal property must be reported if the percentage of rent for personal property exceeds 50 percent or if the rent is based on the tenant's profit or income. This reporting is required because these forms of rent are ineligible for the exemption of rental income from unrelated business income taxation. The deductions claimed that are directly connected with these income streams must also be reported.

Another schedule pertains to unrelated debt-financed income. All debt-financed properties owned by the filing exempt organization must be described. Also to be reported is the amount of gross income from or allocable to debt-financed property and the deductions that are directly connected with or allocable to this type of property.

A schedule requires reporting of receipt of interest, annuities, royalties, and rent from controlled corporations. This schedule entails reporting with respect to tax-exempt and nonexempt controlled organizations, and the reporting of deductions that are directly connected with these income flows.

A schedule relates to the reporting of investment income of exempt social clubs and certain other tax-exempt organizations. This reporting requires a description of each type of investment income, the amount of those forms of income, the deductions that are directly connected to the generation of the income, and of any amounts set aside for charitable purposes.

A schedule pertains to exploited exempt activity income, other than advertising income. Each exploited activity must be described, along with reporting of gross unrelated business income and the expenses directly connected with production of unrelated business income. Another schedule is where advertising income is reported, broken down between income from periodicals reported on a consolidated basis and those reported on a separate basis. In both instances, the name of the periodical(s) must be reported, along with gross advertising income, direct advertising costs, circulation income, and readership costs.

Still another schedule is where the compensation of trustees, directors, and officers is reported, from the standpoint of the unrelated business rules. These individuals and their titles must be identified, along with the percentage of time each of them devotes to business and the amounts of compensation attributable to unrelated business.

This return is due on or before the fifteenth day of the fifth month following the close of the organization's tax year. For failure to file this tax return in a timely manner, additional tax may be imposed.

Chapter 7
Charitable Giving Rules

The federal income tax charitable contribution deduction rules are integral to an understanding of what it takes to be a successful philanthropist. In some instances, the deduction is not that much of a factor, such as where the amount to be given to charity is much greater than the corresponding deduction can absorb. In many instances, particularly where noncash gifts are involved, the availability of a charitable deduction is a driving factor.

I divide the law of charitable giving into two parts. One part is the *substantive* law, which concerns matters such as whether a transfer is a contribution, the percentage limitations, the deduction reduction rules, and planned giving. The other part is the *administrative* (or maybe a better term is *procedural*) law, pertaining to recordkeeping, substantiation, valuation, and recordkeeping requirements.

Charitable Gifts

The concepts of *gift* and *charitable gift* are discussed in Chapter 4. As noted there, a *gift* is a transfer of money or other property that is voluntary and is motivated by reasons other than an expectation of some financial benefit in return. A *charitable gift* is a gift made to or for the use of a charitable donee.

For our purposes, a *charitable donee* largely means a nonprofit organization that is operated for charitable, educational, scientific, religious, and like purposes (see Chapter 2). But it should be recognized that, for tax law purposes, charitable donees also include certain veterans' groups, fraternal societies, cemetery companies, and governments, such as the U.S., the states, and the District of Columbia.

Gifts of Property

Charitable gifts are commonly made using money—cash, checks, electronic transfers, debit and credit cards, and the like. Matters quickly become more complex where gifts of property are involved, inasmuch as the tax law differentiates between personal property and real property, tangible property and intangible property. The real fun starts when gifts of interests in property come into play. Further complications can arise because there can be disputes over the value of property.

The federal income tax treatment of gifts of property is dependent on whether the property is capital gain property. The tax law makes a distinction between *long-term capital gain* and *short-term capital gain* (although generally a net gain of the latter is taxed as ordinary income). Property that is neither long-term capital gain property nor short-term capital gain property is *ordinary income property*. These three terms are based on the tax classification of the type of revenue that would be generated on sale of the property. Short-term capital gain property is generally treated the same as ordinary income property. Therefore, the actual distinction is between capital gain property (really long-term capital gain property) and ordinary income property.

Capital gain property is a capital asset that has appreciated in value and, if sold, would give rise to long-term capital gain. To result in long-term capital gain, property must be held for a specified period, generally 12 months. Typical forms of capital gain property are stocks, bonds, and real estate.

The charitable deduction for capital gain property is often equal to its fair market value or at least is computed using that value. Gifts of ordinary income property generally produce a deduction equivalent to the donor's cost basis in the property. The law provides exceptions to this "basis-only rule;" an example is a gift by a corporation out of its inventory.

Percentage Limitations

The extent of charitable contributions that can be deducted for a tax year is limited to a certain amount, which for individuals is a function of the donor's *contribution base*—essentially, the individual's adjusted gross income. This level of annual deductibility is determined by six percentage limitations. They are dependent on several factors, principally the nature of the charitable recipient and the nature of the property donated. The examples used here assume an individual donor with an annual contribution base (adjusted gross income) of $100,000.

The first four limitations apply to gifts to public charities and private operating foundations (see Chapters 3 and 5).

First, there is a percentage limitation of 60 percent of the donor's contribution base for contributions of cash. A donor with a $100,000 contribution base may, in any one year, make deductible gifts of this type up to a total of $60,000. If an individual makes contributions that exceed the 60 percent limitation, the excess may be carried forward and deducted in one to five subsequent years.

Second, there is a limitation of 50 percent of the donor's contribution base for contributions of ordinary income property. A donor with a $100,000 contribution base may, in any one year, makedeductible gifts of this type up to a total of $50,000. If an individual makes contributions that exceed the 50 percent limitation, the excess generally may be carried forward and deducted in one to five subsequent years. Thus, if this donor gave $60,000 to public charities in year one and made no other charitable gifts, he or she would be entitled to a deduction of $50,000 in year one, and the $10,000 would be available for deductibility in year two.

The third percentage limitation is 30 percent of the donor's contribution base for gifts of capital gain property. A donor thus may, in any one year, contribute up to $30,000 in qualifying stocks, bonds, real estate, and like property, and receive a charitable deduction for that amount. Any excess (more than 30 percent) is subject to the carryforward rule. If a donor gave $50,000 in capital gain property in year one and made no other charitable gifts that year, he or she would be entitled to a charitable contribution deduction of $30,000 in year one, and the $20,000 would be available in year two.

A donor who makes gifts of cash, ordinary income property, and/or capital gain property to public charities (or private operating foundations) in any one year generally must use a blend of these percentage limitations. For example, if the donor in year one gives $50,000 in ordinary income property and $30,000 in appreciated capital gain property to a public charity, his or her charitable deduction in year one is $30,000 of capital gain property and $20,000 of cash (to keep the deduction within the overall 50 percent ceiling); the other $30,000 of cash is carried forward to year 2 (or years 2 through 5, depending on the donor's circumstances).

The fourth percentage limitation allows a donor of capital gain property to use the 50 percent limitation, instead of the 30 percent limitation, where the amount of the contribution is reduced by the unrealized appreciation in the value of the property. This election is usually made by donors who want a larger deduction in the year of the gift for an item of property that has not appreciated in value to a great extent.

The fifth and sixth percentage limitations apply to gifts to private foundations and certain other charitable donees (other than public charities and private operating foundations). These other donees are generally veterans' and fraternal organizations.

Under the fifth percentage limitation, contributions of cash and ordinary income property to private foundations and other entities may not exceed 30 percent of the individual donor's contribution base. The carryover rules apply to this type of gift. If the donor gives $50,000 in cash to one or more private foundations in year one, his or her charitable deduction for that year (assuming no other charitable gifts) is $30,000, with the balance of $20,000 carried forward into subsequent years (up to year five).

The sixth percentage limitation is 20 percent of the contribution base for gifts of capital gain property to private foundations and other charitable donees. There is a carryforward for any excess deduction amount. For example, if a donor gives appreciated securities, having a value of $30,000, to a private foundation in year one, his or her charitable deduction for year one (assuming no other charitable gifts) is $20,000; the remaining $10,000 may be carried forward.

If more complexity is needed, it is available, in the form of special rules for contributions for conservation purposes. Individuals may deduct the fair market value of a conservation contribution to a public charity to the extent of 50 percent of the contribution base over the amount of all other allowable charitable contributions. These contributions that exceed the 50 percent limitation may be carried forward for up to 15 years. Want more? In the case of an individual who is a farmer or rancher, a contribution deduction for a conservation gift is allowable up to 100 percent of the excess of the individual's contribution base over the amount of all other allowable charitable contributions. Any excess may be carried forward for up to 15 years as a contribution subject to the 100 percent limitation.

Deductible charitable contributions by corporations in any tax year may not exceed 10 percent of pretax net income. Excess amounts may be carried forward and deducted in subsequent years (up to five years). For gifts by corporations, the federal tax laws do not differentiate between gifts to public charities and private foundations. As an illustration, a corporation that grosses $1 million in a year and incurs $900,000 in expenses in that year (not including charitable gifts) may generally contribute to charity and deduct in that year an amount up to $10,000 (10 percent of $100,000); in computing its taxes, this corporation would report taxable income of $90,000. If the corporation instead gave $20,000 in that year, the numbers would stay the same, except that the corporation would have a $10,000 charitable contribution carryforward.

In the case of a corporation, the stock of which is not publicly traded, that is a farmer or rancher, a conservation contribution is allowable up to 100 percent of the excess of the corporation's taxable income over the amount of all other charitable contributions. Any excess may be carried forward for up to 15 years as a contribution subject to the 100 percent limitation.

A corporation that uses the accrual method of accounting can elect to treat a contribution as having been made in a tax year if it is actually donated during the first two-and-a-half months of the following year. Corporate gifts of property are generally subject to the deduction reduction rules, discussed next.

A business organization that is a *flow-through entity* generates a different tax result when it comes to charitable deductions. (These organizations include partnerships, other joint ventures, small business (S) corporations, and limited liability companies.) These organizations, even though they may make charitable gifts, do not claim charitable contribution deductions. Instead, the deduction is passed through to the members or other owners on an allocable basis; they claim their share of the deduction on their tax returns.

Deduction Reduction Rules

A donor (individual or corporation) who makes a gift of *ordinary income property* to any charity (public or private) must confine the charitable deduction to the amount of the cost basis of the property. The deduction is not based on the fair market value of the property; it must be reduced by the amount that would have been gained (ordinary income) if the property had been sold. As an example, if a donor gave to a charity an item of ordinary income property having a value of $1,000, for which he or she paid $600, the charitable deduction would be $600.

Any donor who makes a gift of *capital gain property* to a public charity generally can compute the charitable deduction using the property's fair market value at the time of the gift, regardless of the cost basis and with no taxation of the appreciation (the capital gain inherent in the property). Suppose, however, a donor makes a gift of capital gain tangible personal property (e.g., a work of art) to a public charity and the gift's use by the donee is unrelated to its tax-exempt purposes (see Chapter 6). The donor must reduce the deduction by an amount equal to the long-term capital gain that would have been recognized had the donor sold the property at its fair market value as of the date of the contribution.

Suppose a donee charitable organization disposes of an item of tangible personal property for which a deduction of more than $5, 000 was claimed within three years of the contribution. If the disposition is in the year of the gift, the donor's charitable deduction generally is confined to the basis amount. In the case of a subsequent disposition, the donor must include as ordinary income any amount of the claimed deduction that is in excess of the donor's basis. This recapture rule includes reporting requirements and a penalty for failure to comply.

Generally, a donor who makes a gift of capital gain property to a private foundation must reduce the amount of the otherwise allowable deduction by the appreciation element in the gift property. An individual, however, is allowed full fair market value for a contribution to a private foundation of certain publicly traded stock.

Deduction reduction rules also apply in instances of charitable contributions of intellectual property (such as patents, copyrights, trademarks, and trade secrets) and taxidermy.

Easements

Special federal income tax rules pertain to contributions to charity of real property or interests in real property for conservation purposes. These rules are an exception to the general rule that there is no charitable deduction for contributions of partial interests in property (see below). A conservation contribution has three fundamental characteristics: being a contribution of a qualified real property interest (including easements), to a qualified organization (competent public charities), and exclusively for conservation purposes.

This body of law is the subject of considerable litigation. One area of dispute concerns the requirement that the restriction for conservation purposes must be granted in perpetuity; thus, arrangements where the contributed property may be substituted or its boundaries altered do not qualify for the deduction. A deduction is unavailable where the easement deed is not more restrictive than local law or homeowners' association rules. If a mortgage or other financing of the property is involved, there is no deduction unless the mortgagee subordinates its rights in the property to the right of the charitable donee to enforce the conservation purpose. A deduction may be denied where the open space or historic preservation requirements necessary for a conservation contribution were not met. Deductions for gifts of easements on golf courses are likely to be denied.

Charitable deductions in this context may be defeated if the easement or other restriction lacked value, such as a situation where the easement restrictions were no greater than criteria imposed by a landmark district. An easement may lack value, for charitable deduction purposes, because an appraisal showed that it inherently did not reduce the value of the property it ostensibly encumbered. A transaction involving the transfer of an easement to a charitable organization may not yield a charitable deduction because of the value of the consideration the transferor received in the exchange.

Other Special Gift Rules

Congress has been busy in recent years in creating charitable giving rules for specific types of property, introducing in the process considerable complexity as to the law of charitable giving. Consider, for example, the law on charitable gifts of intellectual property (patents, copyrights, trademarks, trade names, and the like). Contributions of this type of property are initially subject to the rule where the charitable deduction is confined to the donor's basis in the property (see foregoing discussion). In this context, however, additional charitable deductions (up to 12) arise equal to various percentages of net income (from 10 to 100 percent) that flows to the charitable donee. The donee must provide certain information to the IRS and the donor.

As another illustration, special rules apply with respect to charitable gifts of vehicles, such as automobiles, boats, and airplanes. Here, the amount of the charitable deduction depends on the nature of the use of the vehicle by the donee organization. If the charitable organization sells the vehicle without any significant intervening use or material improvement of the vehicle, the amount of the deduction cannot exceed the gross proceeds received from the sale. These rules are accompanied by extensive substantiation requirements and penalties.

A donor may take a deduction for a charitable contribution of a fractional interest in tangible personal property as long as the donor satisfies the general deduction requirements and, in subsequent years, makes additional charitable contributions of interests in the same property. Recapture of the income and gift tax charitable deductions can occur under certain circumstances, such as where the donor's remaining interest in the property is not contributed to the same donee within 10 years or where the donee does not timely take substantial physical possession of the property or use the property for an exempt purpose.

Generally, a charitable deduction for a gift of clothing or household items is not allowed unless the gift item is in good used condition or better. A deduction may be allowed for a charitable contribution of an item of clothing or a household item not in good used condition or better if the amount claimed for the item is more than $500 and the donor includes with the tax return a qualified appraisal with respect to the property.

There are even rules pertaining to charitable contributions of taxidermy. The amount allowed as a deduction for a charitable gift of taxidermy property that is contributed by the person who prepared, stuffed, or mounted the property is the lesser of the donor's basis in the property or its fair market value.

A charitable contribution deduction is not available for a gift of services or the use of property.

Partial Interest Gifts

Most charitable gifts are of all ownership of a property—the donor parts with all right, title, and interest in the property. A gift of a *partial interest* is also possible—a contribution of less than a donor's entire interest in the property.

As a general rule, charitable deductions for gifts of partial interests in property, including the right to use property, are not available. The exceptions are for gifts of an outright remainder interest in a personal residence or farm; gifts of an undivided portion of one's entire interest in a property; gifts of a lease on, option to purchase, or easement with respect to real property granted in perpetuity to a public charity exclusively for conservation purposes; and a remainder interest in real property granted to a public charity exclusively for conservation purposes.

Contributions of income interests in property in trust are basically confined to the use of charitable lead trusts. Aside from a charitable gift annuity and gifts of remainder interests, there is no charitable deduction for a contribution of a remainder interest in property unless it is in trust and is one of three types: a charitable remainder annuity trust, a charitable remainder unitrust, or a pooled income fund.

Planned Giving

There are two basic types of planned gifts. One type is a legacy: under a will, a gift comes out of a decedent's estate (as a bequest or devise). The other type is a gift made during a donor's lifetime, using a trust or other agreement.

These gifts once were termed *deferred gifts*, because the actual receipt of the contribution by the charity is deferred until the happening of some event (usually the donor's death). But the term *deferred giving* has fallen out of favor. Some donors (to the chagrin of the gift-seeking charities) gained the impression that it was their tax benefits that were being deferred.

A planned gift usually is a contribution of a donor's interest in money or an item of property, rather than an outright gift of the money or property in its entirety. (The word *usually* is used because gifts using insurance do not neatly fit this definition and because an outright gift of property, in some circumstances, is treated as a planned gift.) Technically, this type of gift is a conveyance of a partial interest in property; planned giving is (usually) partial interest giving.

An item of property conceptually has within it two interests: an *income interest* and a *remainder interest*.

The income interest within an item of property is a function of the income generated by the property. A person may be entitled to all of the income from a property or to some portion of the income—for example, income equal to five percent of the fair market value of the property, even though the property is producing income at the rate of six percent. This person is said to have the (or an) income interest in the property. Two or more persons (such as husband and wife) may have income interests in the same property; these interests may be held concurrently or consecutively.

The remainder interest within an item of property is the projected value of the property, or the property produced by reinvestments, at some future date. Put another way, the remainder interest in property is an amount equal to the present value of the property (or its offspring) when it is to be received at a subsequent point in time.

These interests are measured by the value of the property, the age of the donor(s), and the period of time that the income interest(s) will exist. The actual computation is made by means of actuarial tables, usually those promulgated by the Department of the Treasury.

An income interest or a remainder interest in property may be contributed to charity, but a deduction is almost never available for a charitable gift of an income interest in property. By contrast, the charitable contribution of a remainder interest in an item of property will—assuming all of the technical requirements are met—give rise to a (frequently sizable) charitable deduction.

When a gift of a remainder interest in property is made to a charity, the charity will not acquire that interest until the income interest(s) have expired. The donor receives the charitable deduction for the tax year in which the recipient charity's remainder interest in the property is established. When a gift of an income interest in property is made to a charity, the charity acquires that interest immediately and retains it until such time (sometimes measured by a term of years) as the remainder interest commences. Again, any resulting charitable deduction is available for the tax year in which the charity's income interest in the property is established.

Basically, under the federal tax law, a planned gift must be made by means of a trust if a charitable deduction is to be available. The trust used to facilitate a planned gift is known as a *split-interest trust,* because it is the mechanism for satisfying the requirements involving the income and remainder interests. In other words, the trust is the medium for splitting the property into its two component types of interests. Split-interest trusts are charitable remainder trusts, pooled income funds, and charitable lead trusts.

There are some exceptions to the general requirements on using a split-interest trust in planned giving. The principal exception is the charitable gift annuity, which is based on a contract rather than a trust. Individuals may give a remainder interest in their personal residence or farm to charity and receive a charitable deduction without utilizing a trust. A trust is also not required for a deductible gift of a remainder interest in real property when the gift is granted to a public charity or certain operating foundations exclusively for conservation purposes. Similarly, a donor may contribute a lease on, an option to purchase, or an easement with respect to real property, granted in perpetuity to a public charity or certain foundations exclusively for conservation purposes, and receive a charitable contribution deduction without a trust. A contribution of an undivided portion of one's entire interest in property is not regarded as a contribution of a partial interest in property.

A donor, although wishing to support a particular charity, may be unwilling or unable to fully part with property, either because of a present or perceived need for the income that the property provides or because of the capital gains taxes that would be experienced if the property were sold. The planned gift is likely to be the answer in this situation: The donor may satisfy his or her charitable desires and yet continue to receive income from the property. The donor also receives a charitable deduction for the gift of the remainder interest, which will reduce or eliminate the tax on the income from the gift property. There is no income tax imposed on the capital gain inherent in the property. If the gift property is not throwing off sufficient income, the trustee of the split-interest trust may dispose of the property and reinvest the proceeds in more productive property. The donor may then receive more income from the property in the trust than was received prior to the making of the gift. In other words, there are many advantages to donors served up by planned giving vehicles.

Charitable Remainder Trusts

The fundamental form of planned giving involves a split-interest trust known as the *charitable remainder trust.* The term is nearly self-explanatory: The entity is a trust by which a remainder interest destined for charity has been created. Each charitable remainder trust is designed specifically for the particular circumstances of the donor(s), with the remainder interest in the gift property being designated for one or more charities.

A qualified charitable remainder trust must provide for a specified distribution of income, at least annually, to or for the use of one or more beneficiaries (at least one of which is not a charity). The flow of income must be for life or for a term of no more than 20 years, with an irrevocable remainder interest to be held for the benefit of the charity or paid over to it. The beneficiaries are the holders of the income interests; the charity has the remainder interest.

How the income interests in a charitable remainder trust are ascertained depends on whether the trust is a *charitable remainder annuity trust* (income payments are in the form of a fixed amount, an *annuity*) or a *charitable remainder unitrust* (income payments are in the form of an amount equal to a percentage of the fair market value of the assets in the trust).

The income payout of CRATs and CRUTs generally is subject to a five percent minimum. That is, the annuity must be an amount equal to at least five percent of the value of the property initially placed in the trust. Likewise, the unitrust amount must be an amount equal to at least five percent of the value of the trust property, determined annually. These percentages may not be more than 50 percent. Also, the value of the remainder interest in the property must be at least 10 percent of the value of the property contributed to the trust.

As to the charitable remainder unitrust, there are four variations of them, with the classification dependent on the income payout. The foregoing criteria essentially define the standard charitable remainder unitrust (SCRUT), also known as the *fixed percentage* CRUT. Two types of CRUTs are termed *income-exception* CRUTs. One of these types allows income payments to begin only once a suitable amount of income flows into the trust and then are paid only prospectively—the *net income* CRUT (NICRUT). The other type of CRUT is like the NICRUT, except that this type of trust can make payments that can be make-up (or catch-up) payments made to make up for income deficiencies in prior years—the *net income make-up* CRUT (NIM-CRUT). The fourth type of CRUT allows for a one-time conversion of a trust from NICRUT or NIMCRUT status to a SCRUT; this is quaintly referred to as the *flip* CRUT (or, if you want to get further mired in acronyms, the FLIPCRUT).

Consequently, one of the decisions for the philanthropist, as a donor to a CRUT, is selection of an income type. Some individuals like the security of fixed income and thus choose the annuity. Others are content to be subject to market fluctuations and pick the CRUT option. If donated property is not generating income at the time of the gift, the donor should choose either the NICRUT or NIMCRUT model.

All categories of charitable organizations—both public charities and private foundations—are eligible to be remainder beneficiaries of as many charitable remainder trusts as they can muster. The amount of the charitable deduction will vary for different types of charitable organizations, however, because of the percentage limitations (see above).

Often, a bank or similar financial institution serves as the trustee of a charitable remainder trust. The financial institution should have the capacity to administer the trust, make appropriate investments, and timely adhere to all income distribution and reporting requirements. It is not unusual, however, for the charitable organization that is the remainder beneficiary to act as trustee. If the donor or a related person is named the trustee, the *grantor trust* rules may apply: The gain from the trust's sale of appreciated property is taxed to the donor.

Conventionally, once the income interest expires, the assets in a charitable remainder trust are distributed to the charitable organization that is the remainder beneficiary. If the assets (or a portion of them) are retained in the trust, the trust will be classified as a private foundation, unless it can qualify as a public charity (most likely a supporting organization) (see Chapter 5).

Recordkeeping Rules

In the case of a charitable contribution of money, irrespective of the amount, applicable recordkeeping requirements are satisfied only if the donor maintains, as a record of the contribution, a bank record or a written communication from the donee showing the name of the donee organization, the date of the contribution, and the amount of the contribution.

For this purpose, a *bank record* includes canceled checks, bank or credit union statements, and credit card statements. Contributions of *money* include those made in cash or by check, electronic funds transfer, credit card, or payroll deduction. For payroll deduction purposes, the donor should retain a pay stub, a wage statement (Form W-2), or other document furnished by the employer showing the total amount withheld for charity, along with the pledge card showing the name of the charity.

For contributions of property other than money, a corporate or individual donor must obtain a receipt from the charitable donee and a reliable written record of specified information about the donated property. The receipt must include the name of the donee, the date and location of the contribution, and a detailed description of the property (including its value). A receipt is not required where the gift is made in circumstances where it is impractical to obtain a receipt, such as when a donor drops off used clothing at a charity's receiving site after business hours.

A donor of property that has appreciated in value must maintain a *reliable written record* of the following specified information for each item of property:

- The name and address of the charitable donee
- The date and location of the contribution
- A detailed description of the property (including the value of the property) and, in the case of securities, the name of the issuing company, the type of security, and whether it is regularly traded on a stock exchange or in an over-the-counter market
- The fair market value of the property at the time of the gift, the method utilized in determining the value, and a copy of the report signed by the appraiser
- The cost or other basis of the property if it is ordinary income property or another type of property where the deduction must be reduced by the gain
- Where the gift is of a remainder interest or an income interest, the total amount claimed as a deduction for the year because of the gift, and the amount claimed as a deduction in any prior year or years for gifts of other interests in the property
- The terms of any agreement or understanding concerning the use or disposition of the property—any restriction on the charity's right to use or dispose of the property, a retention or conveyance of the right to the income from the donated property, or an earmarking of the property for a particular use.

Additional rules apply to charitable gifts of property other than money for which the donor claims a deduction in excess of $500. The donor is required to maintain additional records showing how the property was acquired and the property's cost or other basis, if it was held for less than six months prior to the date of gift. For property held for six months or more preceding the date of contribution, the cost or other basis information should be submitted by the donor if it is available.

These rules apply with respect to small gifts. They are superseded for larger gifts by the two bodies of law discussed next.

Gift Substantiation

The federal tax law contains several charitable gift substantiation rules. Under this body of law, donors who make a separate charitable contribution of $250 or more in a year, for which they claim a charitable contribution deduction, must obtain written substantiation from the donee charitable organization if the gift is to be deductible.

More specifically, the rule is that the charitable deduction is not allowed for a separate contribution of $250 or more unless the donor has written substantiation from the charitable donee of the contribution in the form of a contemporaneous written acknowledgment. Thus, donors cannot rely solely on a canceled check as substantiation for a gift of $250 or more.

An acknowledgment meets this requirement if it includes the following information: (1) the amount of money and a description (but not value) of any property other than money that was contributed; (2) whether the donee organization provided any goods or services in consideration, in whole or in part, for any money or property contributed; and (3) a description and good-faith estimate of the value of any goods or services involved or, if the goods or services consist solely of intangible religious benefits, a statement to that effect. The phrase *intangible religious benefit* means "any intangible religious benefit which is provided by an organization organized exclusively for religious purposes and which generally is not sold in a commercial transaction outside the donative context." An acknowledgment is *contemporaneous* if the contributor obtains the acknowledgment on or before the earlier of (1) the date on which the donor filed a tax return for the taxable year in which the contribution was made or (2) the due date (including extensions) for filing the return.

Other technical terms abound. The phrase *goods or services* means money, property, services, benefits, and privileges. Certain goods or services, however, are disregarded for these purposes: (1) those that have insubstantial value and (2) certain annual membership benefits offered to an individual in exchange for a payment of $75 or less per year. A charitable organization provides goods or services *in consideration* for a donor's transfer if, at the time the donor makes the payment to the charity, the donor receives or expects to receive goods or services in exchange for the payment. Goods or services a charitable organization provides in consideration for a payment by a donor include goods or services provided in a year other than the year in which the payment was made. A *good-faith estimate* means a charitable organization's estimate of the fair market value of any goods or services, without regard to the manner in which the organization in fact made the estimate.

These rules are taken quite seriously in court, where often charitable deductions involving millions of dollars are eradicated, solely because the acknowledgement document was incomplete or (worse) misleading. In one case, for example, a charitable contribution deduction of $338,080 was lost because the donor did not have the requisite substantiation. In another case, the court voided charitable deductions valued at $64.5 million, where the preparers of the document, in reciting elements of consideration provided to the donors, deliberately omitted reference to a variety of additional material elements.

As noted, the substantiation rule applies in respect to separate payments. Separate payments are generally treated as separate contributions and are not aggregated for the purpose of applying the $250 threshold. In cases of contributions paid by withholdings from wages, the deduction from each paycheck is treated as a separate payment. Congress has provided the IRS with authorization to issue antiabuse rules in this area (addressing practices such as the writing of multiple checks to the same charity on the same date).

The written acknowledgment of a separate gift is not required to take any particular form. Thus, acknowledgments may be made by letter, postcard, e-mail, or computer-generated form. A donee charitable organization may prepare a separate acknowledgment for each contribution or may provide donors with periodic (e.g., annual) acknowledgments that set forth the required information for each contribution of $250 or more made by the donor during the period.

The U.S. Tax Court held that the requisite substantiation language can be found in a gift agreement. A series of documents evidencing a bargain sale was ruled to adequately satisfy these substantiation rules. This court has also held that a deed, in this case a conservation easement deed, may satisfy the substantiation requirements. The easiest way to satisfy the requirements in this fashion, of course, is where the deed contains the requisite language. The court has also held, however, that, when a deed does not include the explicit statement, the deed as a whole may determine if the donee provided goods or services in exchange for the contribution. Factors that support this compliance are that the deed recites no consideration other than preservation of the property and that the deed states that it constitutes the entire agreement of the parties. The properly executed deed in another case did not contain the requisite language nor did it meet the *as a whole* test. Suitable substantiation was found in a letter signed by a government official. It has been held, however, that a settlement agreement between a donor and a donee cannot serve as an appropriate substantiation document.

The Tax Court has made the administration of this area of the law much more difficult. This is because it held that these rules apply with respect to verbal (unwritten) *expectations* or *understandings* a donor may have with respect to the charitable recipient when making a contribution. This court thus equated, for this purpose, expectations with goods or services. How representatives of charitable organizations are supposed to divine their donors' inner thoughts when giving is not clear.

The substantiation rules get tougher as the amount contributed increases. Thus, there is no charitable deduction for a gift of property, where the claimed deduction is more than $500, unless a description of the property involved is included in the donor's tax return for the gift year. If a charitable deduction of more than $500,000 is clamed, there is no deduction for a gift of property unless the donor attaches a copy of a qualified appraisal (see below) to the tax return for the year. Again, courts are not fooling around in this context. In one instance, a claimed deduction for $64.5 million was denied due to lack of gift substantiation. In these instances, two questions must be asked. Why didn't the charity provide the needed substantiation? Where were the lawyers?

It is the responsibility of a donor to obtain the substantiation and maintain it in his or her records. (Again, the charitable contribution deduction is dependent on compliance with these rules.) A charitable organization that knowingly provides a false written substantiation to a donor may be subject to a penalty for aiding and abetting an understatement of tax liability.

These substantiation rules do not apply to transfers of property to charitable remainder trusts or to charitable lead trusts. The requirements are, however, applicable to transfers to pooled income funds. In the case of these funds, the contemporaneous written acknowledgement must state that the contribution was transferred to the charitable organization's pooled fund and indicate whether any goods or services (in addition to the income interest) were provided in exchange for the transfer. The contemporaneous written acknowledgement, however, need not include a good-faith estimate of the income interest.

Another gift substantiation rule applies in connection with donor-advised funds. A charitable deduction for a gift to a donor-advised fund is deductible only if the sponsoring organization meets certain criteria and the donor obtains a contemporaneous written acknowledgment from the sponsoring organization stating that the organization has exclusive legal control over the contributed assets.

Even where a charitable organization provides a donor with a contemporaneous written acknowledgment in exchange for a contribution, the donor should review it to be certain the document contains all of the required language. Recently, your author received an ostensible substantiation letter from a major university (that presumably has a phalanx of lawyers at its disposal) that states that the "[f]ederal tax law requires us to inform you that no goods, services or privileges were provided in exchange for this donation." First, the federal tax law does no such thing. Second, the law references "consideration," not "exchanges." Third, the statute makes no reference to "privileges." This acknowledgment probably is sufficient to sustain the deduction, but that is a determination each donor (or donor's lawyer) should make—or demand a more precisely phrased substantiation document.

Property Valuation

The law contains requirements relating to proof when charitable deductions for contributions of property are claimed by an individual, a closely held corporation, a personal service corporation, a partnership, or an S corporation. These requirements, when applicable, must be complied with if the deduction is to be allowed.

The requirements apply to contributions of property (other than money and publicly traded securities) if the aggregate claimed or reported value of the property (and all similar items of property for which deductions for charitable contributions are claimed or reported by the same donor for the same tax year, whether or not donated to the same donee) is in excess of $5,000. The phrase *similar items of property* means property of the same generic category or type, including stamps, coins, lithographs, paintings, books, nonpublicly traded stock, land, or buildings.

For each gift of this type, the donor must obtain a *qualified appraisal* and attach an *appraisal summary* to the tax return on which the deduction is claimed. For a gift of nonpublicly traded stock, the claimed value of which does not exceed $10,000 but is greater than $5,000, the donor does not have to obtain a qualified appraisal but must attach a partially completed appraisal summary form to the tax or information return on which the deduction is claimed.

A *qualified appraisal* is an appraisal made no more than 60 days prior to the date of the contribution of the appraised property. The appraisal must be prepared, signed, and dated by a *qualified appraiser* and cannot involve a prohibited type of appraisal fee.

Certain information must be included in the qualified appraisal:

- A sufficiently detailed description of the property
- The physical condition of the property (in the case of tangible property)
- The date (or expected date) of contribution

- The terms of any agreement or understanding concerning the use or disposition of the property
- The name, address, and Social Security number of the qualified appraiser
- The qualifications of the qualified appraiser
- A statement that the appraisal was prepared for tax purposes
- The date or dates on which the property was valued
- The appraised fair market value of the property on the date (or expected date) of contribution
- The method of valuation used to determine the fair market value
- The specific basis for the valuation
- A description of the fee arrangement between the donor and the appraiser

The qualified appraisal must be received by the donor before the due date (including extensions) of the return on which the deduction for the contributed property is first claimed. If a deduction is first claimed on an amended return, the appraisal must be received before the date on which the return is filed.

One qualified appraisal for a group of similar items of property contributed in the same tax year is acceptable, as long as the appraisal includes all of the required information for each item. If a group of items has an aggregate value appraised at $100 or less, the appraiser may select these items for a group description rather than a specific description of each item.

The appraisal summary must be on IRS Form 8283, signed and dated by the donee and qualified appraiser (or appraisers), and attached to the tax return on which the donor is first claiming or reporting the deduction for the appraised property. The signature by the donee does not represent concurrence in the appraised value of the contributed property.

Certain information must be included in the appraisal summary:

- The name and taxpayer identification number of the donor
- A sufficient description of the property
- A summary of the physical condition of the property (in the case of tangible property)
- The manner and date of acquisition of the property
- The basis of the property
- The name, address, and taxpayer identification number of the donee
- The date the donee received the property

- The name, address, and taxpayer identification number of the qualified appraiser (or appraisers)
- The appraised fair market value of the property on the date of contribution
- A declaration by the qualified appraiser

The rules pertaining to separate versus group appraisals apply to appraisal summaries. A donor who contributes similar items of property to more than one charitable donee must attach a separate appraisal summary for each donee.

If the donor is a partnership or an S corporation, it must provide a copy of the appraisal summary to every partner or shareholder who is allocated a share in the deduction for a charitable contribution of property described in the appraisal summary. The partner or shareholder must attach the appraisal summary to his or her tax return.

The *qualified appraiser* declares on the appraisal summary that he or she holds himself or herself out to the public as an appraiser; because of the competencies described in the appraisal, he or she is qualified to make appraisals of the type of property being valued. The appraiser also states that he or she understands that a false or fraudulent overstatement of the value of the property described in the qualified appraisal or appraisal summary may subject the appraiser to a civil penalty for aiding and abetting an understatement of tax liability, and consequently the appraiser may have appraisals disregarded.

An individual is not a qualified appraiser if the donor had knowledge of facts that would cause a reasonable person to expect the appraiser to falsely overstate the value of the donated property. The donor, donee, or certain other related persons cannot be a qualified appraiser of the property involved in the transaction. (In formulating these rules, the government did not include in the criteria certain professional standards or the establishment of a registry of qualified appraisers.) More than one appraiser may appraise donated property, as long as each appraiser complies with the requirements.

Generally, no part of the fee arrangement for a qualified appraisal can be based on a percentage (or set of percentages) of the appraised value of the property. If a fee arrangement is based in any way on the amount of the appraised value of the property that is allowed as a charitable deduction, it is treated as a fee based on a percentage of the appraised value of the property. (In certain circumstances, this rule does not apply to appraisal fees paid to a generally recognized association that regulates appraisers.)

These rules are *directory* rather than *mandatory*. This means that the *doctrine of substantial compliance* applies. In applying this doctrine, the courts look at whether the government's requirements relate to the substance of the status. If so, strict adherence to all statutory and regulatory requirements is necessary. One court held that these appraisal substantiation requirements "do not relate to the substance or essence of whether or not a charitable contribution was actually made."

These administrative rules can have an unwanted interrelationship with the substantive rules relating to the charitable deduction. For example, a donor of a conservation easement claimed a charitable deduction for the year in which the deed was executed, only to be told by a court that the deduction was not available for that year because it had to be postponed to the following year inasmuch as that was the year in which the deed was recorded. But the deduction for the following year, as it turned out, was unavailable because by then the appraisal associated with the gift had become stale!

Reporting Requirements

The annual information return filed by the larger charities (Form 990, Schedule M) imposes a battery of reporting rules on charitable organizations that receive noncash contributions. Considerable information is sought by the IRS about gifts of art, automobiles, intellectual property, real estate, and other types of property.

If a charitable organization donee sells or otherwise disposes of gift property within three years after receipt of the property, it generally must file an information return (Form 8282) with the IRS. Copies of this information return must be provided to the donor and retained by the donee.

This information return must include the name, address, and taxpayer identification number of the donor and the donee; a detailed description of the property; the date of the contribution; the amount received on the disposition; and the date of the disposition.

A donee that receives from a corporation a charitable contribution valued in excess of $5,000 generally does not have to file a donee information return.

Chapter 8
Putting It All Together

With the information in the prior chapters at hand and understood, we are now ready to work together and make you the best and most successful of philanthropists. All you need to do is follow a mere 20 rules.

Factors to Consider

But, before reviewing the rules, let's collect the relevant factors you need to consider:

- The amount of money or the value of other property you have to contribute to charity.
- The charitable activity or activities which you wish to fund.
- Whether you want to institutionalize your position as a philanthropist.
- Whether you want a board of directors and, if so, its size.
- Whether you want to be a director and/or officer of a charity.
- Your need or desire for control over the charity or charities you will be funding.
- Whether you want employment opportunities for yourself and/or one or more family members.
- Your need or desire for one or more types of charitable contribution deductions.
- Whether you will be contributing property other than money and publicly-traded securities.
- Whether you want to fund legislative and other advocacy activities.

- Whether you want to have a supporting organization.
- Whether you want your charity to have a for-profit subsidiary.
- Whether you want or need to engage in fundraising.
- If so, whether the fundraising efforts will involve seeking grants from private foundations.
- Whether you want an income flow as the result of your giving.

Rules to Follow

Application of the 20 rules that follow amounts to mixing and matching the foregoing 15 factors.

Rule #1: Charity Predominates

The paramount rule is to do your charitable thing. Whether you have $1,000 or $100 million to give to charity, the most important part is to fund the cause or causes you are most passionate about. (I concede that the closer to $100 million you can get, the more fun you will have. You will also have more work.) Again, your legal framework within which to determine your charitable goals is the subject of Chapter 2. Whether it is fighting poverty, banishing a disease, working for health care law reform, or tackling urban blight, go for it. Institutionalizing the process, charitable deductions, employment, personal recognition, and all of that will follow in due course. Once you get your charitable juices flowing, the tax law (and I) will take you the rest of the way.

Reality must intrude here. Obviously, the less money (or other property) you have to work with, the more constrained your giving options will be. You are not going to be the founder of a hospital with $1,000. (You can't even get your name on a metal plate on the back of a hospital's chair for that sum.) So, at that level of giving, you have these choices: give the money to your favorite charity (e.g., one of your local hospitals), invest the money so you will have more to give later (after payment of capital gains taxes), or wait around hoping to win a lottery or receive a large bequest and then contemplate a larger gift.

Rule #2: It's (Almost) All About Control

When the potential for some serious charitable giving is presented, the likelihood arises that the erstwhile donor will start thinking about creating one or more charitable entities that will receive the gifts (sometimes termed *donees*). And when that type of thinking gets underway, my experience is that the matter of control will soon surface. Humans seem to want to control what they create. The entrepreneurial spirit has intersected with philanthropy.

Let's say you want to start a charity. (Do not worry at this point about whether your charity is to be public or private and all of that.) Do you want to create the entity, put your millions into it, become its executive director, build the organization's program base over a nice span of years—and then have someone take it all away from you? I don't think so.

Most individuals who start charities want to maintain control over them—or at least they think about it. I help individuals start nonprofit organizations all the time, and this matter of control always arises early in the process. It is normal. (This phenomenon also occurs when a for-profit business is being contemplated.) It is certainly possible for you to create and control a charity. But there are trade-offs, which we will explore momentarily.

Please know that the IRS doesn't like nonprofit organizations that are controlled by a few individuals. There is nothing unlawful about entities of this nature, and nothing immoral or unethical either. The IRS, being the IRS, will always be suspicious that something nefarious is taking place or soon will be. Again, the doctrines of private inurement or private benefit loom. The IRS loves to apply these bodies of law (to the detriment of the organizations involved, of course); the agency does so almost weekly.

Here is some bad news I hate to deliver: The IRS's policy is that a governing board of a charity that is small (and/or that consists of individuals who are related) is automatically evidence of private benefit, thus precluding the organization of tax exemption. (The IRS does not apply this policy to private foundations, fearing a national upheaval in protest.) But, I also have good news: The IRS is wrong.

In this connection, the IRS relies heavily on a case involving an organization by the catchy name of Bubbling Well Church. I bring this up because the IRS dearly loves this case and thus cites it frequently. Or, in some instances, mis-cites it. The church wasn't forthcoming with the IRS, dodging questions during the process of attempting to secure recognition of tax exemption. It failed to acquire exemption for this reason. The church's board consisted entirely of members of one family. The court said that fact meant that the organization should be subject to greater scrutiny. The IRS sometimes cites this case in support of the (wholly untenable) proposition that a governing board of a charitable organization consisting of related persons is automatically evidence of private benefit.

In some instances, the IRS will go further. IRS rulings have the agency saying that the boards of public charities must have a majority of "independent" (unrelated, unpaid) directors or that the board must be "reflective of the community" or that this type of board must be the subject of "public oversight." Don't let the IRS agent get away with this nonsense. If the agent persists, bring in a lawyer, if one isn't already serving.

Rule #3: If you want control, you must pick your structure

If you want to control a for-profit company, how do you do it? You own a majority, if not all, of the company's stock. That is termed an *equity interest* in the company. You can't, however, have an equity interest in a charity. Well, you can, but if you do, it will not be tax-exempt, because owning equity in a nonprofit organization is a form of private inurement. So, to have control of a charity, you need to figure out a way to do that without the ownership feature.

The main way to control a charity—and the easiest way—is to have at least a majority of the members of the governing board. A few states allow one-director boards; that structure drives IRS agents into apoplexy, and thus I advise against that approach (unless you have a charitable trust, but even then I counsel involvement of other trustees). The vast majority of the states require at least three directors, so I would start with that number. To make this control feature work, the directors other than you must be individuals you trust. That is, you trust them to not run off with the charity and the fruits of your multi-year labors. (Founders do get ousted from time to time; just ask Travis Kalanick)

So Mary Mack decides to form a charity, which she will control. Ms. Mack becomes an initial board member. She picks as two other board members her husband, Peter, and their only son, Paul. Peter, Paul, and Mary Mack decide to round out the board by adding their close friends Bob Dean and Harriet Deluca. (Peter, Paul, and Mary and Dean & Deluca, that's one heck of a board!) As long as these individuals are trustworthy from Mary's standpoint, Mary controls the charity. This board can them become a *self-perpetuating* board, which means that the board members reelect themselves or elect their successors. (Most states require terms of office.)

A variant of this approach is to use *ex officio* positions. For example, Mary can structure the charity's board (this is reflected in the articles of organization or the bylaws) so that the charity's president, secretary, and treasurer are automatically also board members. (Contrary to the understanding of some, board members who are there because of an ex officio position can vote.) All Mary has to do, for example, is see that she is elected President of the charity, Peter is elected Treasurer, and Paul is elected Secretary.

Another approach, which I recommend sparingly, is the membership feature. An individual can be the sole member of a charity. (This feature works best, however, where the member is another charitable organization.) The member then selects the board members and the officers of the charity. Although lawful, the IRS, ever suspicious and assuming the worst, will not be too keen on use of this control mechanism.

Rule #4: If you want to institutionalize your charitable giving, pick one or more of four options

If you want to do more than simply give money to existing charities, that is, you want to have a charity of your own, you have three choices: a public charity, a private foundation, or a donor-advised fund. Actually, you have a fourth option: a combination of the foregoing three choices.

If having a charity "of your own" is your goal, and you want name recognition, any of these choices is available. Assume your name is Thomas Crowe. You can establish the Thomas Crowe School for Gifted Children (a public charity), the Thomas Crowe Foundation (a private foundation), or the Thomas Crowe Charitable Fund (a donor-advised fund). With respect to the School, there can be the Thomas Crowe Supporting Foundation (a supporting organization) and/or the Thomas Crowe Endowment Fund (perhaps a supporting organization).

Rule #5: If you want name recognition but not institutionalization, make a naming gift

An existing charitable hospital may be constructing a building or a university constructing another dormitory. If you give enough, your name can also be the building's name. With a nonprofit theater, you can give and have your name on a metal plate affixed to a chair. Name recognition on a chair is not as spectacular as name recognition on a tall building, but it isn't as expensive either.

Rule #6: If you want control, you probably want a private foundation

Clearly, under the law, individuals can control a private foundation. Indeed, most private foundations are controlled in this manner, many by members of the same family. Yes, theoretically, you can control a public charity such as a school or church, but in real life that is not likely to happen. You can't control a supporting organization (not formally anyway), and you certainly can't control a donor-advised fund.

Rule #7: If your main interest is maximized charitable deductions, you probably want a public charity

As has been said repeatedly, the charitable contribution deduction rules favor gifts to public charities. The percentage limitations in the case of contributions to public charities are much more favorable. Gifts of property, the more appreciated in value the better, generate much bigger deductions when made to public charities than when made to private foundations. The type of public charity or charities you select will be governed by the rules that follow.

Rule #8: If you don't have that much to give (relatively speaking), and want some institutionalization, your choice is probably a donor-advised fund

It does not cost that much to create a donor-advised fund with your name on it. You can add money to the fund if you wish. From the standpoint of grantees, transfers from your fund look just like private foundation grants. There is no law setting a minimum or maximum amount for contributions to a donor-advised fund (although a sponsoring organization may have a policy as to the minimum). For that matter, there is no law as to minimums or maximums as to funding of private foundations either (although start-up and ongoing operating costs will have a bearing as to the minimum). What is the minimum amount that should be contributed in forming a private foundation? No one knows. As a practical matter, the minimum should be $500,000, perhaps $1 million.

Rule #9: If you want to give property other than money or publicly traded securities, and the property has significantly appreciated in value, you undoubtedly want to give to a public charity

Once again, the charitable deduction rules favor gifts to public charities. Aside from the more favorable annual percentage limitations, gifts of appreciated property generate larger charitable deductions than gifts of the property to private foundations. Gifts of property other than public securities to private foundations must have the deductible amount confined to the donor's basis in the property. When the same gift is made to a public charity, usually the deduction is based on the full fair market value of the property. Also, gifts of property to private foundations can give rise to excess business holdings problems (see next rule).

Rule #10: If you want to give your business to charity, the donee (assuming it agrees to accept the gift) probably should be a public charity

Some donors contemplate charitable contributions of a business they formed and built up over the years. Charities are usually skittish (or should be) about accepting gifts of businesses because they rarely want to continue running the business and are fearful (or should be) that they won't be able to sell the business. If a donee can be found, however, it probably will be a public charity. Private foundations have limits as to the business interests they can own, without incurring penalty taxes. A special rule, however, protects foundations from excess business holdings taxation for five years where the business is acquired by gift or bequest. A very special rule allows the IRS to grant an additional five years to dispose of a gifted business under certain conditions. Even if this type of gift is to a public charity, however, if the gift is of a corporation's stock and the stock is that of an S corporation, the income generated by the stock and the capital gain occasioned on the sale of the stock will be unrelated business income.

Rule #11: Gifts of tangible personal property should be carefully made

Donors should be cautious when giving tangible personal property to charity. Why? Because where the property is put to a use that is unrelated to the recipient charity's exempt purpose ,the charitable deduction is confined to an amount that is equal to the donor's basis in the property. That is, the deduction in this situation cannot be based on the fair market value of the donated property. Thus, for example, the gift of a valuable, highly appreciated painting to a museum is likely to be more deductible than the gift of the same property to a hospital.

Rule #12: If you want to support attempts to influence legislation, you probably want to use a public charity

Public charities live under less onerous rules, when it comes to efforts to influence enactment or preventing enactment of legislation, than private foundations. They can attempt to influence a legislative process—engage in lobbying—as long as those activities are not substantial. As discussed (see Chapter 5), the rules as to measurement of allowable lobbying can be tricky. Private foundations can make general support grants to public charities that engage in lobbying as long as money is not earmarked for legislative efforts or it is not otherwise obvious that lobbying is being funded. Also, private foundations can utilize various exceptions in this context, such as the self-defense exception, the exception for the provision of technical advice, and the "exception" for educational activities.

Rule #13: If you want to utilize a supporting organization, an eligible public charity must be involved

Many reasons call for use of a supporting organization, such as placement of one or more programs, fundraising efforts, or an endowment in a separate entity. Since private foundations cannot be supported organizations; use of a public charity in this context is mandatory. This is the case irrespective of whether the putative supported organization establishes the supporting organization or the supporting organization is being created at the behest of you, the philanthropist. Difficulties lie with respect to Type III supporting organizations, so caution there is warranted. An organization sponsoring donor-advised funds can have a supporting organization, although the impetus for doing so is not likely to come from a donor to a donor-advised fund.

Rule #15: If you want to utilize a for-profit subsidiary, a public charity must be selected

Public charities can have for-profit subsidiaries. Private foundations cannot, because of the excess business holdings rules—unless the subsidiary receives only passive income.

Rule #16: If fundraising is to be undertaken, the charity most likely will be a public one

Some charitable organizations want to engage in fundraising, to enhance or supplement their financial circumstances, such as schools and theaters. Other charitable organizations have fundraising efforts because they are inherently of necessity with respect to their existence and public charity status. Private foundations rarely engage in fundraising, content to live on their investment income (and avoid charitable fundraising regulation). A private foundation with a solid and ongoing fundraising program would cease to be a private foundation!

Rule #17: Think about using more than one charitable entity

It may make sense to have more than one charitable entity in the picture. This may be done to take advantage of the charitable deduction rules. As noted, gifts of some forms of property are more deductible if made to a public charity than to a private foundation. Or another example is use of a public charity to engage in advocacy efforts. There is nothing in the law that prevents an individual or a group of individuals from controlling and contributing to more than one charitable organization.

Rule #18: Think about integrating your charitable activities with your personal financial plans

There is more to charitable giving, from a law standpoint, than generating charitable contribution deductions. Those deductions help with finances, to be sure, but don't overlook ways to give to charity and get income as a result. I am thinking primarily here about a charitable remainder trust. A charity you create (public or private) can be the remainder interest beneficiary of this type of trust. So, if more personal income is of interest, take some of the money you would otherwise contribute to charity and transfer it to a remainder trust instead. The gift principal will ultimately go to your charity anyway; in the interim, you can have some annuity or unitrust income flowing your way (and obtain some professional money management in the bargain).

Rule #19: Think about integrating your charitable giving with your estate plan

We have focused on lifetime charitable giving. But charitable giving can be done at and after death. Charities can be funded from decedents' estates; they can be created from estates. Some private foundations are established as trusts pursuant to a provision in a decedent's will; these are termed *testamentary charitable trusts*. Again, one can mix and match. A charity can be established during a lifetime and funded during a lifetime and then funded some more after death. Admittedly, this is easier to do with private foundations than with public charities. But the more money involved, the greater the opportunities to integrate charitable giving with estate planning (and with lifetime financial planning (see the previous rule)).

Rule #20: Charities can convert their tax status or that can happen involuntarily

It does not happen very often, but the tax status of a charitable organization can change. One of the ways this can happen is when an organization loses its public charity status. (Remember the presumption that a charitable organization is a private foundation.) A charitable hospital may sell its assets to a for-profit company, with the entity receiving the sales proceeds becoming a private foundation. A publicly supported charity can falter in its fundraising and lapse into private foundation status. Conversely, a private foundation can convert to, for example, a supporting organization or a school or initiate a fundraising program and convert to a publicly supported charity.

Structural and Operational Scenarios

Here are some fact situations illustrating application of the structural and operational rules.

Carrie

Carrie Sellers has, over the 60 years of her life thus far, accumulated about $75,000 that she can afford to give to charity. When we discussed her situation, I advised her that, as a practical matter, she had two choices: Give the money to one or more of her favorite charities or transfer the money to a donor-advised from which grants to the charities of her choice could be made (assuming the sponsoring organization followed her advice). Carrie liked the idea of the Carrie Sellers Charitable Fund; she opted to establish a donor-advised fund at her local community foundation. Carrie was still employed at that time, earning $60,000 annually (her total adjusted gross income). I advised that her annual maximum charitable deductible amount was $30,000 (50% of $60,000). Thus, Carrie can deduct $30,000 of the $75,000 this year, another $30,000 next year, and $15,000 the year after that. I reminded Carrie that she can always make additional contributions to "her" Fund.

Steve and Mary

We met Steve and Mary Smith in Chapter 1. They had liquidated their 20-year business before meeting with me. On that occasion, I learned they wanted to devote the proceeds of the sale, $10 million, to charitable pursuits. Since they had liquidated the business before my involvement, I did not have the opportunity to discuss with them their options of contributing the business assets or the stock in their business corporation to charity (assuming they could find a charity to accept that gift). They brought the same attitude they had about their business to the matter of a charitable organization—they wanted to control it. I mentioned the donor-advised fund approach, knowing they would reject it out of hand, which they promptly did. The same happened with respect to the establishment of a public charity; they didn't have any particular type of charity in mind, such as a school, and were concerned that any board of directors they would have to form would be renegades and run off with the charity. They liked the idea of a private foundation, preferring their control of the charity to the negligible charitable deduction they would receive. When they learned that their daughters, Molly and Polly, could join them on the foundation's board, they were greatly excited. Matters soured when the subject of employment of their daughters by the foundation, as reviewers of grant proposals, came up. I gently pointed out a problem of starting a foundation with only $10 million: the mandatory payout would be a mere $500,000. Distribution of a half million dollars could not justify employment of two fulltime employees. The Steve and Mary Smith Family Foundation was formed; the four of them, as board members and volunteers, decide on the payment of grants.

Peter and Sally

We also met Peter and Sally Brown in Chapter 1. Peter and Sally didn't need too much persuasion to establish a private foundation with their inherited $50 million. They, too, wanted control over their charity and the flexibility of making grants as they wished. We played around with the notion of creating a supporting organization rather than a private foundation, but the lack of control by them scared them away from that approach. The annual payout for the Peter and Sally Brown Foundation will be a minimum of $2.5 million. We believe that that sum is sufficient to justify hiring their daughter, Jessica, as an employee of the Foundation.

Carl and Nancy

And we met Carl and Nancy Jones in Chapter 1. They, too, were quick to conclude that a private foundation was for them. With an annual minimum payout of $5 million, their children, Robert and Priscilla, will, as employees of the Carl and Nancy Jones Foundation, be in charge of the Foundation's grantmaking program. Nancy is taken with the notion of a private operating foundation, which will undertake environmental research. Some of their $100 million may be used to fund this second foundation. Carl and Nancy own some real estate; they may contribute that property to the operating foundation.

I also suggested to Carl and Nancy that they consider placing some of the $100 million, perhaps $5 million, in a charitable remainder trust. This approach may somewhat reduce their overall charitable deductions, although the income tax percentage limitations may operate to deny them deductibility of the entire $100 million. In this way, they can enhance their joint income cash flow.

Roger Fowles

Roger Fowles is a wealthy man, born into and raised by a wealthy family. He is 45, never married. His life passion is antique automobiles; he is an avid collector of them. Roger was referred to me by a client. He wanted to meet, to learn more about the possible use of charitable organizations and techniques of charitable giving.

As he talked about his hobby, it occurred to me that his collection could be—probably should be—housed in a tax-exempt museum. I broached the subject with him; his greatest qualm was giving his cars away. His second greatest reserve was fundraising; his understanding was that charities had to engage in fundraising and he wanted no part of that. I launched into my patter about the differences between public charities (where the museum would likely be a publicly supported charity, with fundraising required) and private foundations (where fundraising generally is not required). I then explained the concept of the private operating foundation, the tax status of many museums, with its more favorable charitable deduction rules. I pointed out that he could lend some of his cars to the museum without charge (which is not self-dealing), then as time went by and he became more comfortable with the arrangement, he could gradually, one vehicle at a time, contribute cars to the museum, garnering tax deductions based on fair market value. Roger followed through on all of this and is now a director and proud chairman of the board of the Fowles Antique Car Museum, which attracts a steady stream of visitors. We are now thinking of converting the museum's tax status to that of a donative publicly supported charity, perhaps initially based on the facts and circumstances test. Roger has become more comfortable with the idea of fundraising, as long as someone else is doing it. We have discussed hiring of a director of development for the foundation. One of these days, I will broach the subject, with Roger, of an endowment fund for the museum, perhaps in a supporting organization.

Paul and Betsy

Years ago, Paul and Betsy Patterson started a public charity, with their own money. Originally, the Patterson Athletic Fund was formed to augment schools' athletic programs, starting with the school then attended by their son, Brian. Grants were made to purchase sports equipment, augment coaches' salaries, and fund scholarships. The Fund grew, to the point that grants were being made throughout the state where the Pattersons live; heavier emphasis on scholarships has evolved. The Fund is a donative publicly supported charity; thus, fundraising is integral to its ongoing public charity status. As of the point in time when the event to be related next occurred, the Fund's annual receipts were about $3 million and its public charity ratio was about 35 percent. Paul and Betsy were approached by a total stranger, Brad, who was impressed with the Fund's programs, so much so that he wanted to contribute $25 million in securities and a parcel of real estate worth $50 million to the Fund. Needless to say, gifts of that magnitude would destroy the Fund's public charity status. Paul and Betsy asked me what to do. I knew the advice couldn't be decline the gift; this couple didn't want the Fund to become a private foundation. For reasons I won't get into, the gifts would not qualify as unusual grants. So, what to do? Answer: Create a Type I supporting organization in relation to the Fund. Call it the Patterson Athletic Endowment. The supporting organization is also a public charity but with no public support requirement, so Brad could make his gifts to the Endowment and claim the maximum in allowable charitable deductions, which he did. Paul and Betsy constructed an office headquarters for the Fund on the land, which the Endowment made available to the Fund at no charge. The securities became the basis for the endowment fund; the Endowment can make grants to the Fund or to the scholarship recipients. Sometimes, two public charities can be better than one.

Walter and Minerva

Walter and Minerva Ashford established a private foundation, the Ashford Foundation. They did this long before we met. The purpose of the Foundation was to make grants to gifted children in furtherance of their education. Unfortunately, Walter and Minerva got caught up, in a negative way, in the private foundation self-dealing rules. It was never clear whether what they were doing was in fact self-dealing; it was borderline in any event. The structure they were entangled in was such that it could not be terminated. I can say no more. They came to me for legal advice. Sometimes when the law is not on your side, the only solution is to change the facts. I suggested bifurcation. (Walter and Minerva were a genteel couple; being unfamiliar with that term, I could see by the looks on their faces they thought I was suggesting an act of perversion.) I recommended that they establish a tax–exempt school (for gifted children, of course). I then recommended that the Foundation be converted into a supporting organization with respect to the school. They did this; the school was named the Ashford Academy and the former private foundation retained its name. Two public charities replaced one private foundation. The self-dealing problem (if there was one) melted away.

Marvin and Delores

Marvin and Delores Dickinson's success with their charity was much along the lines of Paul and Betsy Patterson. The Dickinsons have annually supported their charity, but retirement for the both of them is about five years away; there won't be the household income flow that has been there so far. They asked me for advice. My response was to establish the Dickinson Charitable Trust with their charity being the remainder interest beneficiary, stop giving to their charity, and put their money in the Trust instead. The Trust will be a charitable remainder annuity trust, where additional contributions can be made to it. The Dickinsons will fund the Trust during the five-year period. The Trust will provide them with an annual annuity. At the death of the second of them to die, the assets in the Trust will be transferred to their charity.

Charitable Giving Administrative Rules Scenarios

Here are some fact situations illustrating application of the charitable giving administrative rules.

Claude and Maude

Claude and Maude Perkins established a private foundation with $50 million. Claude and Maude are on the foundation's board, along with their lawyer, Henry. They are also the foundation's officers. No one on the board provided Claude and Maude a gift substantiation letter. For example, Claude didn't write to himself. If the IRS finds out about this omission, no part of the $50 million gift will be deductible under the federal tax law.

Harry and Mary

Harry and Mary Bender contributed a façade easement on their residence to a qualified donee. The neighborhood in which their residence was located had been designated a historic district by the National Register of Historic Places. Based on an appraisal, Harry and Mary claimed a charitable deduction for this gift in the amount of $108,000. The deduction was disallowed by the IRS because this couple failed to include a copy of the appraisal with their tax return, as required by law. A court agreed with the IRS, imposing tax penalties on Harry and Mary for being "careless, if not reckless" in not complying with this law.

Patricia

Patricia Munson, an avid amateur geologist, contributed, in two tax years, a number of fossil trilobites to a qualified public charity. The values claimed for these gifts, for deduction purposes, were $109,800 and $136,500. Both deductions were denied in full by the IRS. Patricia failed to establish that she had obtained qualified appraisals of the gifted fossils. This case was tried before a court; in that proceeding, Patricia sought to introduce into evidence purported appraisals by a qualified appraiser; the court refused to admit them because the appraiser denied having written them.

Moreover, Patricia was unable to meet the substantiation requirements. She secured letters from the charity acknowledging the gifts but failed to notice that they did not state whether the organization provided any goods or services in exchange for the contributions. (It did not.) A court upheld the IRS.

Sam

Sam Mann is an avid collector of aircraft. He contributed an interest in an airplane to a tax-exempt aeronautical heritage society that operates a museum. He claimed a charitable deduction in the amount of $338,080. In connection with gifts of this nature, the charitable donee must provide certain information concerning the gift to the IRS, by means of Form 1098-C; a copy of that form is to be provided to the donor. The donor then can satisfy the substantiation requirement by attaching a copy of the form to the donor's tax return. Sam did not comply with this rule because the society did not prepare and file the form with the IRS. The IRS disallowed this deduction, in part because Sam failed to comply with the substantiation requirement. A court upheld the IRS.

Sheila

Sheila Sanders is a wealthy activist, intensely concerned with restoration and maintenance of historic property. She contributed a façade easement to a public charity specializing in the care and upkeep of historic and conservation properties. Sheila claimed a contribution deduction of $11.4 million for this gift. A few years later, she was audited by the IRS; this charitable deduction was denied in its entirety. Why? The charity was late in recording the deed of easement. She contested this decision of the IRS in court—and lost. The court held that an easement of this nature has no legal effect, under state law, until it is recorded. This tardiness in recording the deed, the court ruled, violated the tax law rule that the gift property be protected in perpetuity.

Derrick

Derrick Martin is a real estate broker, a certified real estate appraiser, and, as a court would characterize him years later, a "prominent entrepreneur." Derrick and his wife, Susan, contributed parcels of real estate, valued at about $20 million, to a charity over a two-year period. Derrick, an entrepreneur to his core, rarely sought advice. He prepared his own tax returns. In connection with these gifts, he prepared the Forms 8283 himself, making many errors and leaving omissions. He did not read the form's instructions; as he would later testify, the form "seemed so clear [to him] that he didn't think he needed to." He prepared his own appraisals, making them unqualified. The IRS took the position that the charitable deductions should not be allowed; the court agreed. The court concluded its opinion with this: "We recognize that this result is harsh—a complete denial of charitable deductions to a couple that did not overvalue, and may well have *undervalued*, their contributions—all reported on forms that even to the Court's eyes seemed likely to mislead someone who didn't read the instructions. But the problems of misvalued property are so great that Congress was quite specific about what the charitably inclined have to do to defend their deductions, and we cannot in a single sympathetic case undermine those rules." Although they can be imagined, Susan's views as to her husband's handiwork as the "defend[er] [of] their deductions" are not known.

George

George Ferris is an aggressive investor. He formed an investor group, then structured it as a limited liability company. The company acquired a remainder interest in property, paying $2.95 million for the interest. Seventeen months later, the company assigned the remainder interest to a major university, claiming a charitable deduction in amount of $33 million. A copy of the requisite Form 8283 was attached to the company's tax return reflecting the deduction, providing the date and manner of its acquisition of the contributed remainder interest. The line on the form for the donor's cost or other adjusted basis was, however, left blank. The IRS denied the charitable deduction because the Form 8283 was not fully completed. The matter went to court, where the IRS prevailed. The court ruled that Congress had required "strict" substantiation requirements. Here, had the form been properly prepared, the court stated, the IRS would have been alerted to the "significant disparity" between the claimed fair market value of the interest and the amount paid by the company to acquire it, and taken action in the face of a "potential overvaluation" of the property. (The court, as part of the process of computing tax penalties, valued the interest at $3.5 million.)

Sandra

Sandra Snyder is the equivalent of Sheila Sanders in terms of the state of her wealth and intensity of passion for the protection and preservation of historic properties. Sandra contributed to a qualified public charity a historic preservation deed of easement pertaining to valuable property. Her claimed charitable deduction, based on a qualified appraisal, was $64.5 million. The charity provided Sandra with a letter acknowledging this contribution. The IRS fully disallowed this gift deduction—because the letter failed to state whether any goods or services were provided to Ms. Snyder in exchange for her gift. (None were.) A court agreed with the IRS.

Note: The foregoing eight scenarios are based on actual court cases, including the amounts of the charitable deductions that were claimed—and lost.

Private Foundations and Donor-Advised Funds

The Philanthropy Roundtable assembled a list of private foundations' uses of donor-advised funds in furtherance of their charitable undertakings. (This list was sent to the Department of the Treasury and the IRS in connection with the development of tax regulations, as noted at the end of Chapter 4.)

The Roundtable wrote that these examples "demonstrate how important donor advised funds can be for private foundations in sustaining our nation's diverse, abundant and vibrant civil society." Donor-advised funds are, the Roundtable added, a "valuable tool for private foundations, which use them for a wide variety of purposes consistent with their purposes and federal law."

Here are some of the illustrations:

Safety and Security
- A private foundation makes grants to a donor-advised fund to support charities in foreign countries where the foundation has staff working in the country, accompanied by their families. Many of these countries are unstable and dangerous; the lives of the foundation's staff and family members would be in jeopardy if this foundation made the grants directly to the charities. This use of a donor-advised fund keeps the identity of the foundation private and protects the safety and well-being of those connected to it.
- A foundation makes grants to a donor-advised fund to support organizations that oppose terrorism, some of which have fatwas against them. This grantmaking protects the foundation's trustees from the threat of violence.

Collaboration Among Foundations
- A foundation utilizes a donor-advised fund at a community foundation as part of a collaborative effort with several other foundations that also make grants to the fund to jointly fund local economic development projects.

This donor-advised fund is a vehicle that can accept and manage grants from multiple sources without the need for establishing an additional management structure for the collaboration.

- A foundation makes grants to donor-advised funds at community foundations in order to participate in multi-foundation collaborative funding efforts, which it finds more efficient than coordinating direct grants by the participating foundations. This approach also allows grantees to have a single entity to which to report .

Support of Local Projects

- A foundation makes grants to a donor-advised fund at a community foundation in a geographic region as to which the foundation lacks significant local knowledge. This grantmaking allows the foundation to access the local knowledge and experience of the community foundation's staff.
- A foundation supports, in collaboration with other foundations, a project collecting data about city and county governments. All of these foundations fund this project at a community foundation.

Funding Outside Normal Areas

- A foundation uses a donor-advised fund when it supports organizations and projects outside of its typical areas of grantmaking.
- A foundation normally does not provide support for fundraising events. The foundation decided to make a one-time exception, funding a major fundraising event for a charity. By granting to a donor-advised fund and recommending a grant to the charity, the foundation avoided sending a signal to other charities that might encourage them to seek a similar funding exception.
- A foundation allows its board members to make discretionary grants. By keeping these gifts private by use of a donor-advised fund, unsolicited proposals from similar organizations, that might otherwise waste time and effort, are reduced.
- A foundation allocates annual grants to a donor-advised fund for innovative programs that are outside the foundation's normal grantmaking procedures. The foundation established a donor-advised fund to be paid out over three years to help drive these programs.

Align Funding With Program Schedule
- A foundation made a grant to a donor-advised fund to support a large capital campaign commitment to a university. The foundation wanted to fund the commitment in a year where its investments performed well, then distribute the funds over several years as elements of the project are completed and the grant contingencies are met.
- A foundation makes grants to donor-advised funds at community foundations because this approach enables the foundation to make distribution decisions with respect to projects based on the projects' timeline and achievements rather than be constrained by the annual distribution requirement.

Maximize Funding and Efficiency
- A foundation uses a donor-advised fund to make international grants to foreign charities. This is seen as a more efficient use of charitable funds inasmuch as the fees are nominal.
- A foundation supports programming at a university's law school that provides training and professional development for federal judges. The organization providing the programming will apply for recognition of exempt status but has yet to do so. The foundation makes grants to a donor-advised fund for this funding, finding this approach more efficient and less costly than making expenditure responsibility grants.
- A foundation used donor-advised fund to support a consumer education project sponsored by a tax-exempt business league. The foundation utilized this approach because a new organization that is administering this project has yet to receive its determination that it is a charitable organization. Again, this avenue of funding was used to avoid more costly and less efficient expenditure responsibility grants.

Instill Family Giving
- A family with a private foundation uses a donor-advised fund to encourage the next generation to be more philanthropic. The family created the fund, with their children as advisors, to provide the children with a giving vehicle. Due to the children's busy lives, this donor-advised fund turned out to be an ideal charitable giving entity enabling the children to learn about funding philanthropy and making an impact, in advance of involving them directly in the management of the foundation.

- A foundation terminated and distributed its assets to a donor-advised fund ton bring multiple generations of family members into the grantmaking process, and document and create the vision for the family's legacy in philanthropy in perpetuity, without the continuing administrative burden of the foundation. This donor-advised fund will become an endowed fund that distributes income each year to causes the family members champion.
- A foundation uses a donor-advised fund during times of economic downturn to maintain granting levels.
- A foundation created a donor-advised fund to create an endowment for an impact investment fund at a university's business school. This investment fund allows students to make investments and learn from the experience.
- A foundation allows its board members to make discretionary grants to a donor-advised fund as to which the foundation is the advisor. By keeping these grants separate from the foundation's general accounts, use of this fund makes accounting easier because the discretionary grant ledger is managed by the sponsoring organization with respect to the fund.
- A foundation allows board members to make discretionary grants, utilizing the due diligence screening capacity of a donor-advised fund sponsor to ensure that the grantees are qualified and have a mission that is aligned with that of the foundation.

The Community Foundation Public Awareness Initiative, consisting of 115 community foundations in 45 states, also submitted comments to the IRS. This group observed that donor-advised funds "have become a vitally important philanthropic tool for [community foundations], their donors, and nonprofit organizations in our communities." It "support[s] changes that will open up more opportunities for charitable giving" and it "oppose[s] any regulations that will discourage charitable giving by making the process more complex for donors, sponsoring organizations, and beneficiary charities to understand."

Conclusion

I wish you the best in giving money and perhaps other property to charity. I hope you experience great pleasure in seeing your money at work, helping those in financial or other need and generally making our world better as a result of your generosity. If you want it, I wish you and perhaps those close to you maximum ongoing control over the charity or charities you have established. I wish you the joy in the resulting large charitable contribution deductions you have created, perhaps freeing up more money for charitable ends. And, perhaps the most important from a lawyer's standpoint, I wish you the peace that comes from avoiding all those legal pitfalls out there that might otherwise have thwarted your objectives. Happy and productive giving!

Additional Resources

If you would like more information about establishing and operating a charitable organization, including a briefing on the applicable federal and state laws, I invite you to explore Hopkins, *Starting and Managing a Nonprofit Organization: A Legal Guide, Seventh Edition* (John Wiley; Hoboken, NJ: 2017).

Should you or your lawyer want more technical and detailed information about the laws pertaining to forming and operating a charitable organization, take a look at Hopkins, *The Law of Tax-Exempt Organizations, Eleventh Edition* (John Wiley; Hoboken, NJ: 2016). This book is annually supplemented.

If you have formed or are otherwise managing or advising a private foundation, you may find helpful Hopkins and Blazek, *The Tax Law of Private Foundations, Fifth Edition* (John Wiley; Hoboken, NJ: 2018). This book, which is annually supplemented, contains detailed chapters on the law concerning private foundations, public charities, and donor-advised funds.

If the focus, by you or your lawyer, is on the charitable giving aspects of being a philanthropist, see Hopkins, *The Tax Law of Charitable Giving, Fifth Edition* (John Wiley; Hoboken, NJ: 2014). This book is annually supplemented.

If your charitable organization is engaged in fundraising, voluntarily or involuntarily, of interest may be Hopkins and Kirkpatrick (now Beck), *The Law of Fundraising, Fifth Edition* (John Wiley; Hoboken, NJ: 2013). This book is annually supplemented.

If you want more information about nonprofit governance, see Hopkins, *Legal Responsibilities of Nonprofit Boards, Second Edition* (BoardSource; Washington, DC: 2009). For more on the law aspects of governance, there is Hopkins and Gross, *Nonprofit Governance: Law, Practices & Trends* (John Wiley; Hoboken, NJ: 2009).

If your charity gets audited by the IRS, you may find a useful companion in Hopkins, *IRS Audits of Tax-Exempt Organizations: Policies, Practices, and Procedures* (John Wiley; Hoboken, NJ: 2008). Not much has changed in the ensuing years.

Overall, if you or your lawyer want to be certain that correct and current terminology is being used in the philanthropic context, see the *Bruce R. Hopkins' Nonprofit Law Dictionary* (John Wiley; Hoboken, NJ: 2015).

For monthly updates on developments in nonprofit law, including public charities and private foundations, and charitable giving, see my newsletter, *Bruce R. Hopkins' Nonprofit Counsel* (John Wiley; Hoboken, NJ). 2018 is its 35th year of publication.

My website is at brucerhopkinslaw.com.

Index